United States
Department of
Agriculture

Forest Service

Northern
Research Station

General Technical
Report NRS-4

Development of Landscape-level Habitat Suitability Models for Ten Wildlife Species in the Central Hardwoods Region

Chadwick D. Rittenhouse
William D. Dijak
Frank R. Thompson, III
Joshua J. Millspaugh

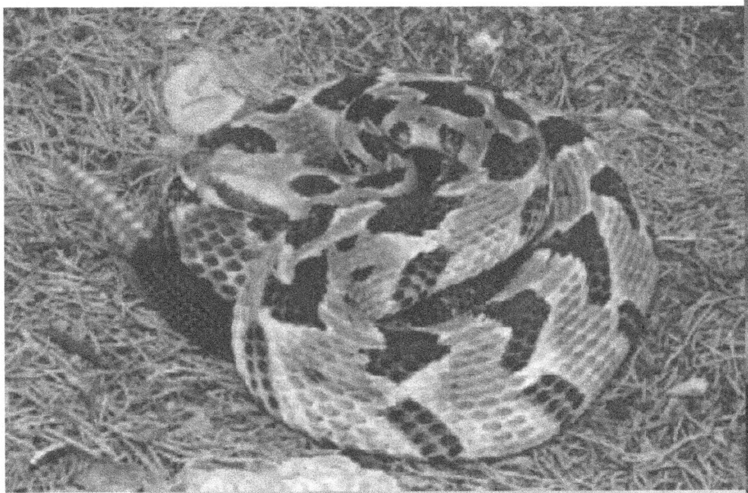

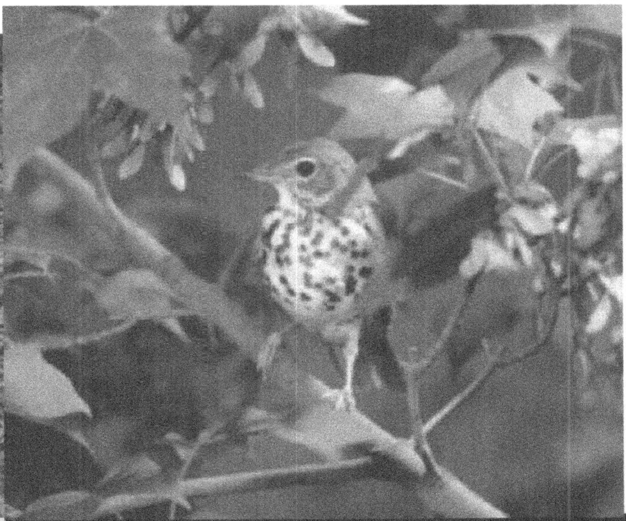

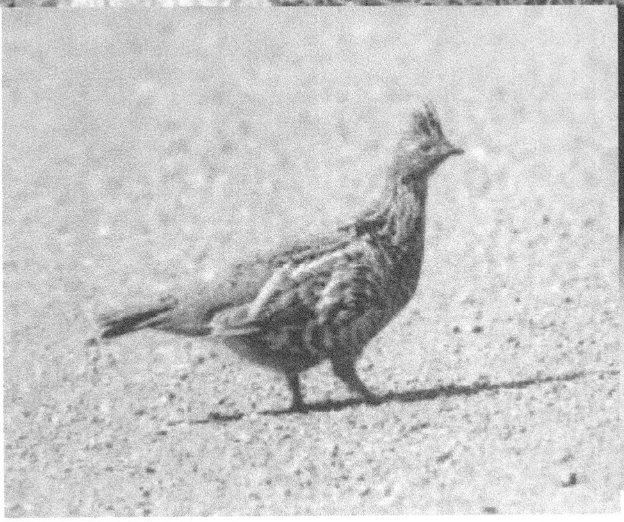

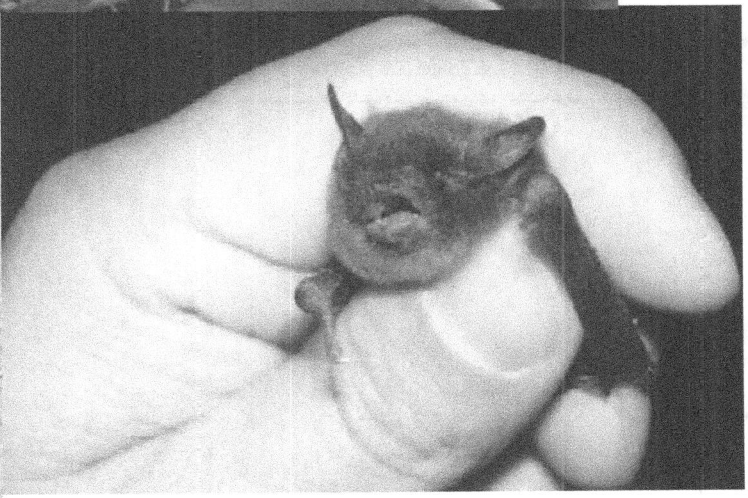

ABSTRACT

Decades of studies on wildlife-habitat relationships have provided important insights into the habitat requisites for many game and nongame species. Many species of conservation or management importance are area or edge sensitive, or need interspersion of habitat requisites to maintain viable populations; however, most habitat suitability models do not incorporate spatial relationships or landscape attributes. Our objective was to develop landscape-level habitat suitability models for 10 species in the Central Hardwoods Region of the Midwestern United States: American woodcock (*Scolopax minor*), cerulean warbler (*Dendroica cerulea*), Henslow's sparrow (*Ammodramus henslowii*), Indiana bat (*Myotis sodalis*), northern bobwhite (*Colinus virginianus*), ruffed grouse (*Bonasa umbellus*), timber rattlesnake (*Crotalus horridus*), wood thrush (*Hylocichla mustelina*), worm-eating warbler (*Helmitheros vermivorus*), and yellow-breasted chat (*Icteria virens*). All models included spatially explicit variables and relationships based on the best available empirical data and expert opinion. We provide an overview of habitat characteristics for each species, discuss the habitat variables used in each model, and provide supporting reference materials for all assumed relationships between quantity of a resource and quality for each species modeled. The models are included in a stand-alone software package, Landscape HSImodels version 2.1, available from the U.S. Forest Service, Northern Research Station (www.nrs.fs.fed. us/hsi). The HSI maps produced by the Landscape HSImodels software are readily displayed within GIS software (e.g., ArcView or ArcGIS). All models may be modified to address site-specific habitat conditions and then applied to other regions. For example, the models may be used to identify priority areas for conservation or management. Additionally, the models may be applied to output from forest simulation software (e.g., LANDIS) and used to evaluate the effects of forest management alternatives in a planning context. As such, these models provide a general approach for evaluating habitat suitability at large spatial scales.

THE AUTHORS

CHADWICK D. RITTENHOUSE, Department of Fisheries and Wildlife Sciences, University of Missouri, 302 Anheuser-Busch Natural Resources Building, Columbia, MO 65211

WILLIAM D. DIJAK, USDA Forest Service, Northern Research Station, 202 Anheuser-Busch Natural Resources Building, Columbia, MO 65211

FRANK R. THOMPSON, III, USDA Forest Service, Northern Research Station, 202 Anheuser-Busch Natural Resources Building, Columbia, MO 65211

JOSHUA J. MILLSPAUGH, Department of Fisheries and Wildlife Sciences, University of Missouri, 302 Anheuser-Busch Natural Resources Building, Columbia, MO 65211

COVER PHOTOS

Top left, timber rattlesnake, courtesy of William E. Peterman, University of Missouri; top right, wood thrush, courtesy of Steve Maslowski, U.S. Fish and Wildlife Service; bottom left, ruffed grouse, USDA Forest Service "find-a-photo:" website; and bottom right, Indiana bat, courtesy of U.S. Fish and Wildlife Service.

Contents

INTRODUCTION

Decades of studies on wildlife-habitat relationships have provided important insights into the habitat requisites for many game and nongame species. Information gained from these studies has been used to develop wildlife habitat models (e.g., habitat suitability index [HSI] models; U.S. Fish and Wildlife Serv. 1980, 1981), the application of which enables assessment of current habitat conditions and predictions of how habitat suitability may change under management (e.g., habitat evaluation procedures; U.S. Fish and Wildlife Serv. 1980, 1981). Radio-telemetry (Rodgers 2001) and computing (e.g., geographic information systems; GIS) technology have enhanced our understanding of wildlife-habitat relationships, especially with regard to wildlife spatial ecology. We now recognize that many species of conservation or management importance are area or edge sensitive, or need interspersion of habitat requisites to maintain viable populations.

Habitat suitability index models (U.S. Fish and Wildlife Serv. 1980, 1981) remain a common approach for assessing wildlife habitat quality (Gustafson et al. 2001, Marzluff et al. 2002, Larson et al. 2003, Larson et al. 2004). Habitat suitability index models evaluate the resource attributes considered important to a species' abundance, survival, or reproduction. Habitat suitability is described by an empirical or assumed relationship between habitat quality and resource attributes on a relative scale that ranges from 0 (not suitable habitat) to 1 (highly suitable habitat) (U.S. Fish and Wildlife Serv. 1980, 1981). The HSI values can be visually presented as habitat suitability maps, which may then be used to make relative comparisons across management alternatives (Gustafson et al. 2001, Marzluff et al. 2002, Larson et al. 2004). Originally, these maps were summarized in terms of habitat units, which is the HSI value multiplied by a unit of area. In this way, habitat units became the currency for evaluating management alternatives in terms of the total amount of habitat lost or gained (U.S. Fish and Wildlife Serv. 1980, 1981; Klaus et al. 2005). However, habitat occupancy depends not only on the HSI values but also on the composition and configuration of habitat units. Thus, the spatial context of wildlife-habitat relationships should be incorporated in HSI models. The use of GIS technology facilitates inclusion of spatially explicit landscape attributes in HSI models.

Our objective was to develop landscape-level, GIS-based HSI models for 10 species in the Central Hardwoods Region of the Midwestern United States (Table 1). The species selected represent a range of habitat requirements (e.g., grassland, forest, disturbance-dependent, and disturbance-sensitive) and management priorities (e.g., game species, Partners in Flight priority species, threatened and endangered species) in the Central Hardwoods Region. We developed the HSI models to evaluate breeding habitat suitability for migratory species and year-round habitat suitability for nonmigratory species. We based all models on the best available empirical data and expert opinion. All models incorporated spatially explicit variables and advances in the understanding of wildlife-habitat relationships

Table 1.—Wildlife species selected for habitat suitability modeling in the Central Hardwoods Region and their management or conservation status

Species	Scientific name	Management or conservation description
American woodcock	Scolopax minor	Disturbance-dependent, migratory game bird
Cerulean warbler	Dendroica cerulean	Late-successional, area-sensitive songbird
Henslow's sparrow	Ammodramus henslowii	Grassland-dependent, area- and edge-sensitive songbird
Indiana bat	Myotis sodalis	Snag- and cave-roosting bat, endangered species
Northern bobwhite	Colinus virginianus	Disturbance-dependent game bird
Ruffed grouse	Bonasa umbellus	Early successional forest-dependent game bird
Timber rattlesnake	Crotalus horridus	Threatened species
Wood thrush	Hylocichla mustelina	Forest-dependent songbird
Worm-eating warbler	Helmitheros vermivorus	Late-successional, fire-sensitive songbird
Yellow-breasted chat	Icteria virens	Disturbance-dependent songbird

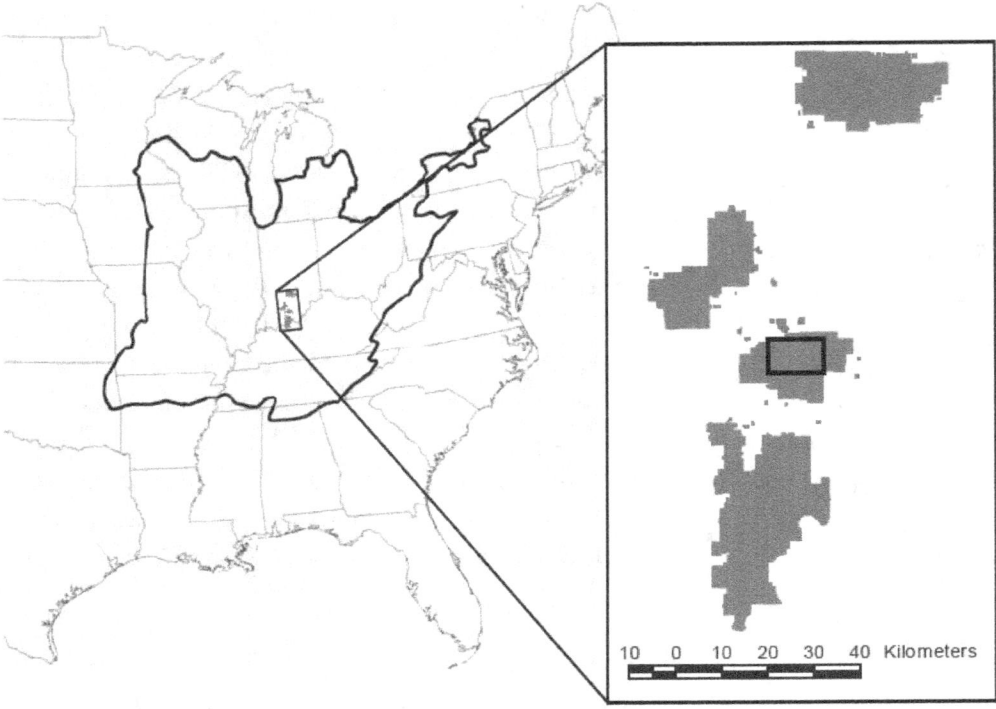

Figure 1.—The Central Hardwoods Region of the Midwestern United States includes the Hoosier National Forest in Indiana. The 4,281 ha display area within the Patoka district is outlined.

since the original models were developed. We provided an overview of important habitat characteristics for each species and discussed the habitat variables chosen for inclusion in the model. We provided supporting reference materials for all assumed relationships between the quantity of a resource and quality for that species. All models developed were included in a stand-alone software package, Landscape HSImodels version 2.1, (Dijak et al. In press) available from the U.S. Forest Service, Northern Research Station (www.nrs.fs.fed.us/hsi).

We purposefully developed HSI relationships for these models based on information available from GIS layers. Additionally, the HSI maps produced by the Landscape HSImodels software are readily displayed within GIS software (e.g., ArcView or ArcGIS). Thus, these models can be used for the evaluation of habitat suitability at large spatial scales. For example we used these models, coupled with appropriate GIS layers of future vegetative conditions under alternative forest management scenarios, to assist land managers and planners in the forest management planning process. Additionally, these models may be modified to address site-specific habitat conditions and then applied to other regions. As such,

these models provide a general approach to evaluating habitat quality and may be used to identify priority areas for conservation or management in addition to the effects of forest management.

METHODS
Area of Applicability and Test Landscape

We developed HSI models for application to the Central Hardwoods Region in the Midwestern United States. Definitions of the Central Hardwoods Region vary; we based our definition largely on Bailey's (1996) ecoregional classification system. We defined the Central Hardwoods Region as the Hot Continental Division (220) within the Humid Temperate Domain, excluding the mountainous portions (M220), and included the eastern portion of the Prairie Division (250) (Bailey 1996). The forested areas within this region are deciduous and contain primarily oak (*Quercus* spp.) and hickory (*Carya* spp.) forests, with some maple (*Acer* spp.), beech (*Fagus* spp.), mixed upland hardwoods, bottomland hardwoods, and lesser amounts of pine (*Pinus* spp.) and cedar (*Juniperus virginiana*). We demonstrated the HSI models on a landscape defined as the Patoka district of the Hoosier National Forest (HNF, Fig. 1). The Patoka district contained approximately

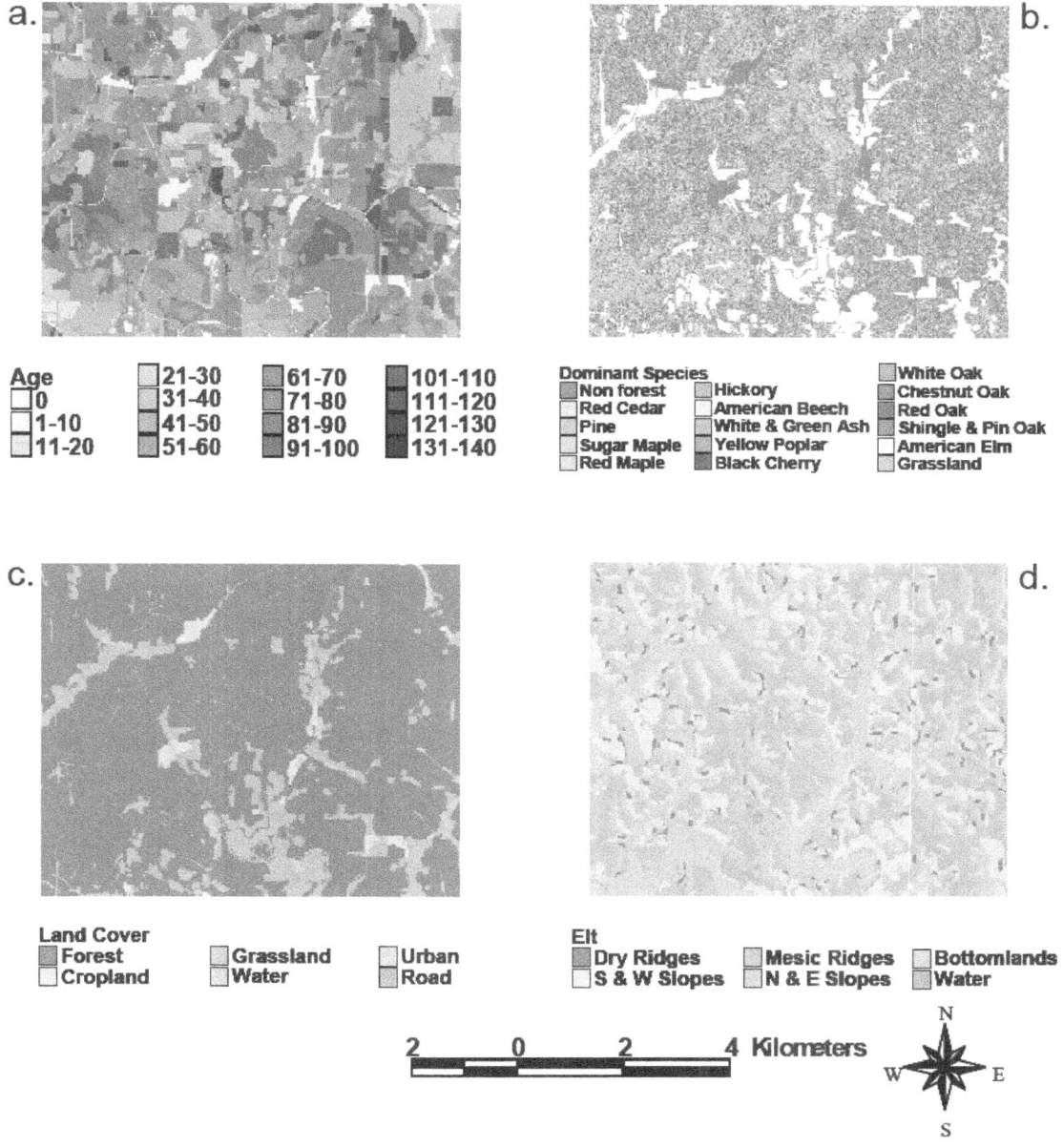

Age
0
1-10
11-20
21-30
31-40
41-50
51-60
61-70
71-80
81-90
91-100
101-110
111-120
121-130
131-140

Dominant Species
Non forest
Red Cedar
Pine
Sugar Maple
Red Maple
Hickory
American Beech
White & Green Ash
Yellow Poplar
Black Cherry
White Oak
Chestnut Oak
Red Oak
Shingle & Pin Oak
American Elm
Grassland

Land Cover
Forest
Cropland
Grassland
Water
Urban
Road

Elt
Dry Ridges
S & W Slopes
Mesic Ridges
N & E Slopes
Bottomlands
Water

2   0   2   4 Kilometers

Figure 2.—Primary input data for landscape-level HSI models developed for the Central Hardwoods Region. Information included tree age (a), dominant overstory species (b), land-cover type (c), and ecological land type (d).

26,868 ha. However, we restricted all figures presented to a smaller, 4,281 ha portion of the Patoka district (hereafter, test landscape) for optimal display resolution using a cell size of 10 m.

Primary Input Data

The HSI models required four different raster-based maps of information (Fig. 2): tree age, species of the dominant overstory trees, ecological land type, and land-cover type. Additional raster-based maps required

for some of the species models will be explained within individual species account. Tree age and species information for the initial forest conditions may be obtained from forest inventories, interpreted from aerial photographs, or derived from satellite imagery (e.g., remote sensing). We used Forest Inventory Analysis (FIA) data, the HNF's inventory database, land-use and land-cover data, and Indiana GAP data to establish current forest conditions for the test landscape. We assigned tree ages (Fig. 2) for stands located on public lands by

Table 2.—Dominant overstory tree species (or species group) classifications for the Central Hardwoods Region

Species Code	Name	Species / Description
1	Nonforest	cropland, urban areas, roads, or water
2	n/a	species code not used
3	Eastern red cedar	*Juniperus virginiana*
4	Pine	*Pinus echinata* and *P. strobus*
5	Sugar maple	*Acer saccharum*
6	Red maple	*Acer rubrum*
7	Hickories	*Carya* spp.
8	American beech	*Fagus grandifolia*
9	White and green ash	*Fraxinus americana* and *F. pennsylvanica*
10	Yellow poplar	*Liriodendron tulipifera*
11	Black cherry	*Prunus serotina*
12	White oak	*Quercus alba*
13	Chestnut oak	*Q. prinus*
14	Red oaks	*Q. rubra, Q. falcata, Q. velutina,* and *Q. coccinea*
15	Shingle and pin oak	*Q. imbricaria* and *Q. palustris*
16	American elm	*Ulmus americana*
17	Grassland	cool or warm season grassland, pasture, or hay fields

Table 3.—Ecological land type codes and descriptions for the Central Hardwoods Region

Code	ELT	Description
1	Dry ridges	Summit or upper shoulder slope positions with ridgetops generally narrower than 75 m and slope gradient <15%.
2	South and west slopes	Backslope positions with generally south aspect and slope gradient >15%.
4	Mesic ridges	Summit or upper shoulder slope positions with broad, flat ridgetops generally wider than 75 m and slope gradient <15%.
5	North and east slopes	Backslope positions with generally north aspect and slope gradient >15%.
6	Bottomlands	Bottomland positions along minor stream valleys and floodplains of minor streams
7	Water	Water

subtracting the year of stand origin from the year of analysis (2003). We identified 14 different dominant overstory tree species (or species groups) and included two additional overstory types, nonforest and grassland, for a total of 16 different dominant overstory species (Table 2, Fig. 2). We used ecological land types (ELT) derived from 10-m Digital Elevation Model (DEM) layers[1]. The ELT coding followed Van Kley et al. (1994) and grouped types by slope, aspect, and relative moisture (Table 3, Fig. 2).

We classified land-cover type for public lands using the HNF forest type codes and for private lands using the land-use land-cover data digitized by the School of Public and Environmental Affairs, Indiana University, for the HNF, cross-referenced with the Indiana GAP data. The HNF forest type codes distinguished between 12 types of closed and open canopy forests or clearcuts, as well as croplands, grasslands (i.e., grassland, pasture, or hay fields), water, urban areas, and wetlands. We collapsed the HNF forest type codes into six general land-cover types:

[1]Created by Guafon Sho, Purdue University

1) forest; 2) croplands; 3) grasslands; 4) water; 5) urban areas; and 6) roads (Fig. 2) for use in the HSI models.

GIS Methods and Spatial Relationships

We modeled some wildlife species considered area or edge sensitive, or that use multiple habitat types to meet life-history requirements. Because these spatial relationships were common to many of the species' models, we present the methodology for them here and address other requirements as needed within species-specific models. Area-sensitive species require a minimum area of contiguous habitat (i.e., a minimum patch size) for occupancy or breeding. We addressed minimum area requirements in two steps. First, we used a suitability index (SI) to identify cells containing suitable habitat based on tree age, tree species, ELT, or land-cover type. We used a patch-definition algorithm to aggregate cells of suitable habitat that were adjacent (i.e., horizontally, vertically or diagonally) to other cells of suitable habitat. Once aggregated, we then used a second SI to assign values to pixels based on the size of the habitat patch in which they occurred.

Edge-sensitive species may experience adverse effects due to edges, such as reduced survival, nest success, or nest density near habitat edges (Donovan et al. 1997, Winter et al. 2000, Woodward et al. 2001). In contrast, species such as the northern bobwhite (*Colinus virginianus*) use woody edges adjacent to croplands or grasslands as escape cover (Roseberry and Klimstra 1984, Williams et al. 2000). Thus, edge effects may be positive or negative, depending on the species. We defined a habitat edge as a change in land-cover type (i.e., grassland to cropland) or tree age (i.e., early successional forest to mature forest). We addressed edge sensitivity using two different approaches: a distance algorithm and a moving-window analysis. The distance algorithm assigned SI values based on the distance of a cell to a habitat or landscape feature (i.e., roads) that defined a habitat edge. Because the distance algorithm assigned an SI value to each cell within the landscape, it was often the most computationally intensive step in the HSI models. We used a moving window for edge sensitivity when the effect was limited to adjacent cells; otherwise, we used the distance algorithm. The moving-window analysis

adjusted the suitability of cells adjacent to habitat edges. For example, the Henslow's sparrow (*Ammodramus henslowii*) is a grassland species that is sensitive to woody edges (Winter and Faaborg 1999, Winter et al. 2000, Bajema and Lima 2001). We applied the moving window to a previous SI that identified patches of suitable grassland habitat. If the center cell of the moving window contained suitable grassland habitat and any cell within the radius of the window contained non-grassland habitat (e.g., forest, urban areas, or roads), the SI value of the center cell was reduced. In other words, a cell containing habitat that was otherwise suitable for Henslow's sparrows had reduced suitability due to the cell's proximity to nonsuitable habitat. We also used the moving-window analysis to assign suitability based on the composition or interspersion of habitats needed for life history requisites.

Some wildlife species have different habitat needs for different activities, such as foraging habitat separate from nesting habitat or escape cover. We used a moving-window analysis to assess the proportion of different habitat requisites within a defined area, typically the average home range size for a species. For example, northern bobwhites nest in grasslands, forage in cropland, and use woody edges for escape cover (Stoddard 1931, Roseberry and Klimstra 1984, Roseberry and Sudkamp 1998, Williams et al. 2000). We applied the moving window to previous SIs that identified suitable grassland, cropland, and woody edges, respectively. We recoded each habitat type (e.g., grassland = 1, cropland = 2, and woody edges = 3) and determined the proportion of each of these three habitat requisites contained within the moving window. We assigned SI value based on the ideal proportion of these three habitat requisites. If all three habitat requisites were present within the window in the ideal proportion, the SI value of the center cell of the window was greatest (SI = 1.00). Otherwise, the SI value was reduced based on the difference between the ideal proportion and the observed proportion. If the window did not contain one of the three habitat requisites, the center cell received SI = 0.00. The final HSI value represented the composite habitat-specific SI values modified by the SI for composition.

MODEL DEVELOPMENT AND APPLICATION

Modeling Philosophy

These models were developed for the explicit purpose of assessing habitat suitability of large geographic areas (>1000 ha) at relatively high resolution (≤30 m cell size). Within the species-specific accounts, we defined suitable habitat as either breeding habitat or year-round habitat. The primary sources of information for these HSI models were extensive literature reviews and expert opinion. When available we used empirical data in the development of suitability relationships; however, the HSI approach in general is less reliant on empirical data for model application than approaches such as resource selection functions (Manly et al. 2002). In this way, HSI models may be applied to large landscapes without labor-intensive field data collection.

Wildlife species experts participated in all stages of model development including literature summaries, initial model development, model review and refinement, and final model approval. A Species Viability Evaluation Panel (SVE Panel) included species experts from state and federal agencies, the scientific research community and nongovernmental organizations. The group convened in 2002 as part of the Hoosier National Forest land management planning process to summarize relevant literature on habitat requirements and population status for species of conservation concern within the Central Hardwoods Region. Following this meeting we conducted additional literature reviews and created the initial HSI models. We presented the HSI models to the SVE Panel in January 2004. The SVE Panel suggested minor revisions to the avian species models and extensive revisions to the Indiana bat (*Myotis sodalis*) and the timber rattlesnake (*Crotalus horridus*) models. We incorporated all model revisions suggested by the SVE Panel. The SVE Panel approved all models in April 2004.

American Woodcock

Overview

The American woodcock (*Scolopax minor*) is a migratory game species confined to North America. Woodcocks breed in the eastern United States north to the boreal forest of Canada and winter in the southeastern United States (Keppie and Whiting 1994). Woodcock habitat requirements vary by gender, time of day, and season. During the breeding season, young to mid-age forests provide feeding and diurnal roosting sites for both sexes and nesting sites for females (Keppie and Whiting 1994). At night, males use open areas for display habitat and both sexes use open areas for nocturnal roosting sites. During the nonbreeding season, woodcocks use a variety of forests, including bottomland hardwoods and upland mixed pine-hardwoods (Keppie and Whiting 1994). An existing HSI model used small-shrub cover, large-shrub cover, sapling density, and basal area to identify woodcock diurnal habitat (Straw et al. 1986). Other studies on American woodcocks indicate that forest and mixed forest, agriculture, and developed areas provide habitat for nesting and brood rearing, feeding, and displaying (Keppie and Whiting 1994). Size of openings and the interspersion of forested and open areas are also important habitat features (Klute et al. 2000).

HSI model

We developed an American woodcock HSI model for breeding and migration habitat in the Central Hardwoods Region. The first suitability index (SI_1) identified tree species suitable for nest sites and diurnal cover. While on the wintering grounds woodcock use a variety of forests, including upland mixed pine-hardwoods and mature longleaf pine that recently has been burned (Keppie and Whiting 1994). During breeding and migration, woodcock primarily use young deciduous forests for diurnal cover. We set $SI_1 = 0.00$ if the dominant tree type was pine, cedar, nonforest, or grassland, and $SI_1 = 1.00$ otherwise. This designation zeroed out grasslands and nonforest areas that may be used for diurnal or roosting habitat. However, we assigned value to grasslands as display and roosting habitat in SI_3. Therefore, the contribution of grasslands to the overall habitat suitability was retained in the model.

In the second suitability index (SI_2), we assigned suitability based on tree age and ELT. American woodcock use deciduous forests for nesting, foraging, and diurnal roosts (Keppie and Whiting 1994). Young to mid-age forests interspersed with openings provide nest sites and young brood habitat (Keppie and Whiting 1994). Woodcock also nest and rear broods in field/forest

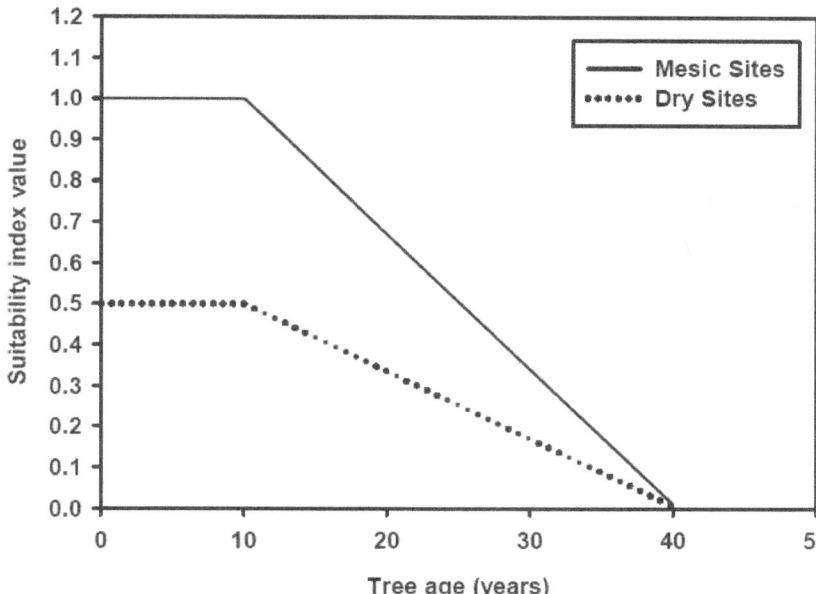

Figure 3.—American woodcock habitat suitability as a function of stand age and ecological land type. Suitability value (SI_2) on mesic sites (mesic ridges, north and east slopes, and bottomlands) = 1.00 at maximum (solid line). Suitability value (SI_2) on dry sites (dry ridges and south and west slopes) = 0.50 at maximum (dashed line).

edges (Murphy and Thompson 1993). Young hardwoods and mixed woods with shrubs adjacent to openings provide moist ground for daytime feeding and diurnal cover (Hudgins et al. 1985, Keppie and Whiting 1994). Hudgins et al. (1985) characterized diurnal sites as having lower elevation and slope than random sites, possibly due to factors affecting food availability. In upland areas, sites used by young broods had greater soil moisture than nest sites (Murphy and Thompson 1993). We grouped ELTs to account for the influence of moisture on sites used by woodcocks. Mesic ridges, north and east slopes, and bottomlands constituted the mesic ELTs, and dry ridges and south and west slopes the dry ELTs. We assigned maximum suitability (SI_2 = 1.00) to stands 1-10 years of age on mesic sites and SI_2 = 0.00 to stands >40 years of age (Fig. 3). We used linear regression to assign suitability to stands 11-40 years of age:

$$SI_2 = 1.33 - 0.033 \times age$$

where *age* is the dominant tree age for a cell. For stands on dry ELTs, we multiplied the age function by 0.5 to reduce suitability value.

In the third suitability index (SI_3), we identified open areas suitable for display, roosting, and nesting habitat. Male woodcock use open areas, including abandoned agricultural fields, forest gaps and cuts, meadows, pastures, orchards, bogs, and other natural clearings for aerial courtship displays (Keppie and Whiting 1994). Both male and female woodcock also use open areas for night roosts, but some woodcock remain in diurnal cover (e.g., forested) at dusk (Krohn 1971, Wishart and Bider 1976) and some females move to different forested cover at dusk (Sepik and Derleth 1993). Female woodcock nest in hawthorn and crabapple fields (Liscinsky 1972) and shrubby old fields (Murphy and Thompson 1993). We assigned value to all cells 0-10 years of age based on ELT. For mesic ELTs, we assigned SI_3 = 0.30 and for dry ELTs we assigned SI_3 = 0.10. All cells with trees >10 years of age received SI_3 = 0.00. Because SI_3 assigned value to all cells 0-10 years of age, including cells containing roads or urban areas, we used SI_4 to zero out these nontarget open areas. We assigned $SI_4 = SI_3$ for grassland, cropland, and forest, otherwise SI_4 = 0.00. Therefore, suitability of open areas = SI_4.

In the fifth suitability index (SI_5), we assigned value based on the interspersion of young- to mid-age forest (SI_2) and open areas (SI_4). Klute et al. (2000) compared known woodcock habitat to random areas using buffers of multiple spatial scales and found that used sites had higher interspersion of water, wetlands, and deciduous forest, with less agricultural and developed lands. Vegetative structure (e.g., tree density, basal area, edge height) and opening size also can be used to characterize breeding habitat (Gutzwiller et al. 1983). The median distance between diurnal sites and singing grounds of singing males was 364 m (range = 50-964 m) in Pennsylvania (Hudgins et al. 1985), which is comparable to studies in Maine (Dunford and Owen 1973, Sepik and Derleth 1993). The quality of singing grounds may be determined by surrounding nesting and brood-rearing cover (Dwyer et al. 1983) because females do not move young broods far from the nest (Sepik et al. 1993) and nests often are located near display sites (Murphy and Thompson 1993). We used a moving window with a 200-m radius, which corresponds to the median distance between diurnal sites and singing grounds and the average total home range size (15 ha, range 0.3-171 ha) for male woodcock in Pennsylvania (Hudgins et al. 1985). The ideal proportion of nesting, foraging, and display habitat is approximately 80 percent nest/forage (forest) to 20 percent display (open).[2]

The final habitat suitability value was the geometric mean of 1) maximum of $SI_1 \times SI_2$ (nesting and foraging) and SI_4 (display); and 2) SI_5, the interspersion of these habitats:

$$HSI = \sqrt[2]{(\max((SI_1 \times SI_2), SI_4) \times SI_5)}$$

Application to test landscape

The first suitability index identified deciduous forest with interspersion of open areas (Fig. 4). The second suitability index, which assigned value based on tree age and ELT, identified numerous forest patches with stands 1-40 years of age. The amount and type of disturbance (e.g., fire, wind, and harvest) greatly influenced the suitability of deciduous forest. Suitability index 3 assigned value to all cells <10 years of age, including roads and urban areas, for display habitat. Suitability index 4 reclassified SI_3 and retained only grasslands, croplands, and young forest as display habitat. Suitability index 5 revealed areas with high interspersion of forest and open areas. The final HSI map reflected the locations of young forest and open areas.

Cerulean Warbler

Overview

The cerulean warbler (*Dendroica cerulea*) is a neotropical migratory bird that breeds in eastern North America and winters in northern South America. In North America, this species is found from April to September in large tracts of mature and second-growth forests with tall deciduous trees (Hamel 2000a). Because no previous HSI model existed for cerulean warblers, we developed a new model based on reported ecological relationships gathered from an extensive literature review.

HSI model

We developed a cerulean warbler HSI model for breeding habitat in the Central Hardwoods Region. The first suitability index (SI_1) identified suitable tree species for breeding habitat. Cerulean warblers use a variety of tree species for nesting throughout their range, including maple (*Acer* spp.), American beech (*Fagus grandifolia*), ash (*Fraxinus* spp.), black walnut (*Juglans nigra*), tulip poplar (*Liriodendron tulipifera*), oak (*Quercus* spp.), and elms (*Ulmus* spp.) (Table 3b in Hamel 2000b). Hamel (2000b) noted that G. Vanderah[3] located nests in pine trees in southern Illinois. However, Robbins et al. (1989) found a negative relationship between relative abundance of cerulean warblers and coniferous canopy cover in the Middle Atlantic states. Without published information on the use of conifers for breeding habitat, we identified only deciduous trees as suitable. We believe this restriction provided a conservative estimate of breeding habitat suitability. We accomplished this by evaluating the dominant tree type for each cell and setting $SI_1 = 0.00$ if the dominant tree type was pine or cedar, and $SI_1 = 1.00$ otherwise.

In the second suitability index (SI_2), we assigned habitat quality based on forest age and ELT. Cerulean warblers breed in mature and second-growth forests with tall deciduous trees (Hamel 2000a). Habitats include wet bottomland, mesic slope, or upland (Hamel 2000b), ranging in elevation from 30-1000 m (Hamel 2000a), though cerulean warblers may occur in greater densities in floodplains or other mesic conditions (Lynch 1981, Garber et al. 1983, Kahl et al. 1985, Robbins et al. 1992). Historical accounts indicate that cerulean warblers were found in both old-growth bottomland forests (Widmann 1895a, 1895b, 1897) and upland forests

---

[2] S. Backs, Indiana Department of Natural Resources, pers. comm.

[3] Illinois Natural History Survey, pers. comm. with Hamel, May 1993

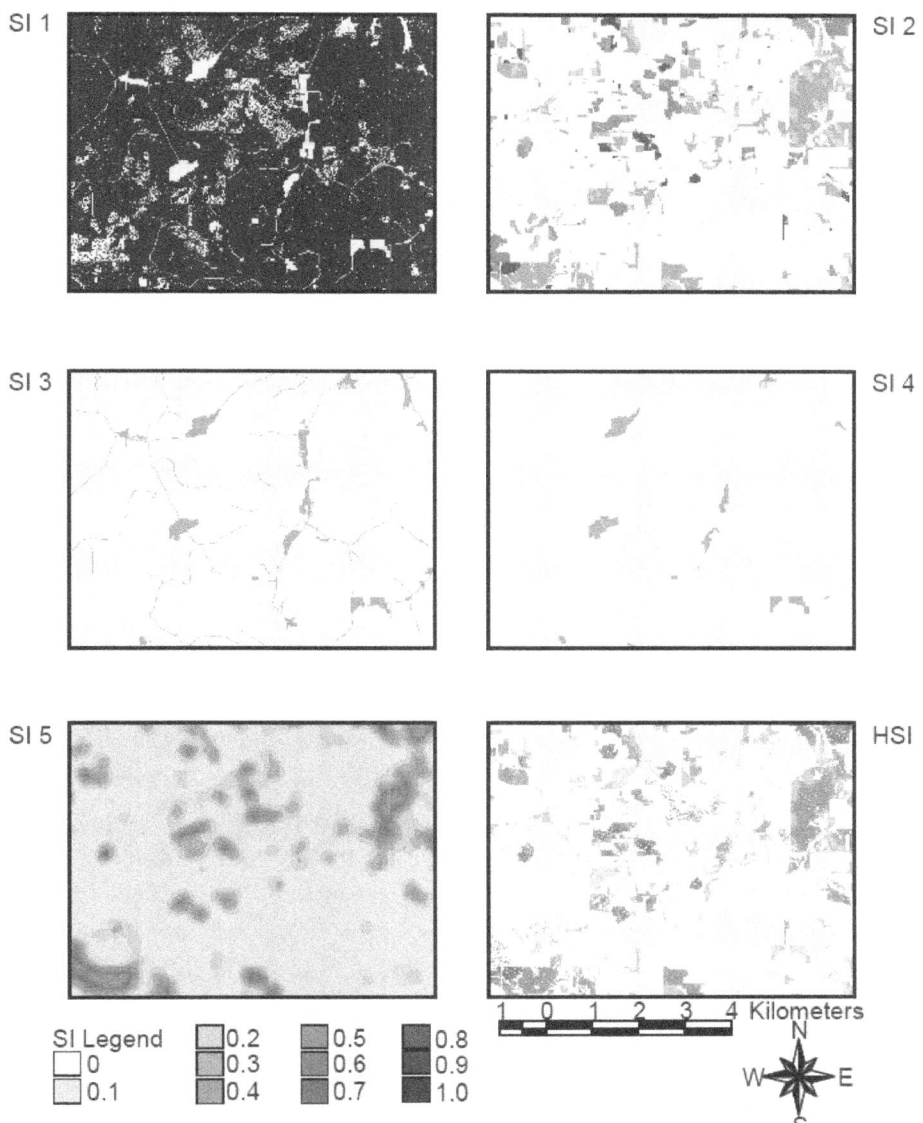

SI 1 SI 2 SI 3 SI 4 SI 5 HSI

SI Legend
0
0.1
0.2
0.3
0.4
0.5
0.6
0.7
0.8
0.9
1.0

1 0 1 2 3 4 Kilometers

N
W—E
S

Figure 4.—American woodcock habitat suitability for a 4,281-ha portion of the Hoosier National Forest, Indiana.

(Todd 1893, Torrey 1896, Schorger 1927). Presently, cerulean warblers often are associated with bottomland or floodplain forests, but this association may be due to the current forest distribution patterns and not necessarily due to a preference for bottomland over upland forest (Hamel 2000b). Recent studies indicate cerulean warblers use upland habitats and ridgetops as frequently as bottomland habitats (Rosenberg et al. 2000, Weakland and Wood 2002, Bosworth and Wood 2003, Nicholson 2003).

In the U.S. Fish and Wildlife Service (USFWS) Region 3, which includes the northern edge of the Central

Hardwoods Region, cerulean warblers were more numerous in riparian bottomland forest (40 percent of birds detected) than mesic uplands (28 percent) or dry upland forest (21 percent) (Rosenberg et al. 2000). Within the Central Hardwoods Region, cerulean warblers use both upland and bottomland forests. Rosenberg et al. (2000) observed cerulean warblers in mesic upland, bottomland and lake margin habitats, and dry upland forest in Indiana. In southern Indiana, Basile and Islam (2001) reported almost exclusive use of ridges, but in earlier successional forest stages. In Ohio, cerulean warblers are associated with dry oak-hickory woodlots, mixed mesophytic forests, wet beech maple woodlands,

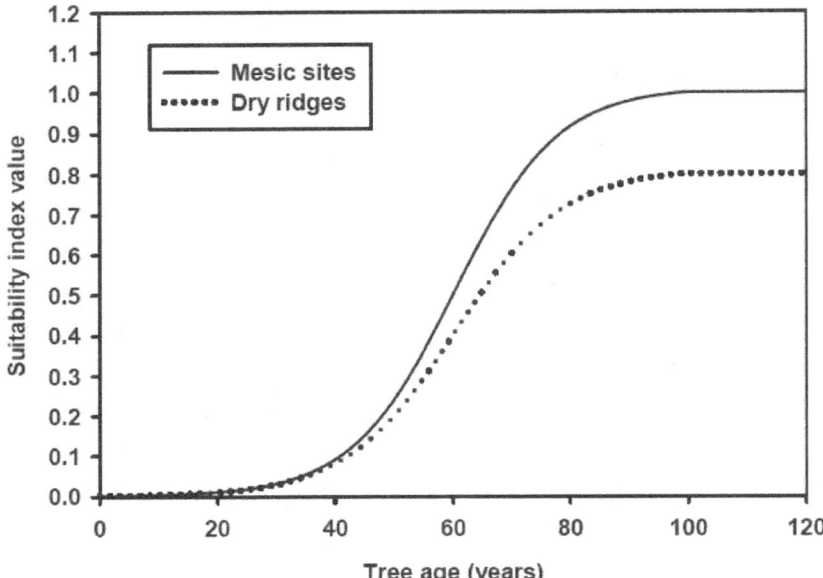

Figure 5.—Cerulean warbler habitat suitability for breeding as a function of stand age and ecological land type. Suitability value (SI_2) on mesic sites (mesic ridges, north and east slopes, and bottomlands) = 1.00 at maximum (solid line). Suitability value (SI_2) on dry ridges = 0.80 at maximum (dashed line).

and extensive floodplain forests (Peterjohn and Rice 1991). In western Kentucky, cerulean warblers are found in mature, relatively undisturbed deciduous forests (Mengel 1965).

We used two different functions to assign suitability to trees on mesic and dry sites (Fig. 5). For trees on mesic sites, which included mesic ridges, north and east slopes, and bottomlands, we subjectively assigned a suitability value based on the equation:

$$SI_2 = \frac{1.0104}{\left(1 + e^{((-treeage-60.1799)/8.7242)}\right)}$$

We developed this equation by fitting a sigmoid function with SI_2 = 0.01 at 20 years of age, SI_2 = 0.50 at 60 years of age, and SI_2 = 1.00 for ≥100 years of age. For trees on dry ridges, we subjectively assigned a suitability value based on the equation:

$$SI_2 = \frac{0.8105}{\left(1 + e^{((-treeage-60.2385)/9.1812)}\right)}$$

We developed this equation by fitting a sigmoid function such that SI_2 = 0.01 at 20 years of age, SI_2 = 0.40 at 60 years of age, and SI_2 = 0.80 for ≥100 years of age. All trees <20 years of age, as well as trees on south and west slopes, received SI_2 = 0.00.

In the third suitability index (SI_3), we established an area requirement by assigning a suitability value based on deciduous forest area (Fig. 6). The cerulean warbler is considered an area-sensitive species. Minimum patch sizes used by individuals varies by region, ranging from 10 ha in Ontario (Hamel 2000a), 20-30 ha in Ohio (Peterjohn and Rice 1991), 700 ha in Middle Atlantic states (Robbins et al. 1989), to 1600 ha in the Mississippi Alluvial Valley in Tennessee (Robbins et al. 1992). Cerulean warbler population surveys conducted in USFWS Region 3 found 65 percent of the birds in patches >400 ha, 25 percent in patches 80-400 ha, and 10 percent in patches <40 ha in size (Rosenberg et al. 2000). Distinguishing between minimum patch size needed for occupancy and minimum patch size needed for breeding is important because the requirements may not be synonymous. In the Middle Atlantic states, 50 percent occupancy occurs at 700 ha, with the maximum probability of occurrence at 3000 ha; however, 700 ha is the minimum area required for breeding (Robbins et al. 1989). Hamel (1992) provided a minimum tract size of 1750 ha, but it is not clear whether the requirement was for occupancy or breeding.

We distinguished between area requirements for occupancy and suitability for breeding. For breeding habitat suitability, we subjectively assigned SI_3 = 0.01 for 100-ha forest patches, SI_3 = 0.10 for 700-ha patches

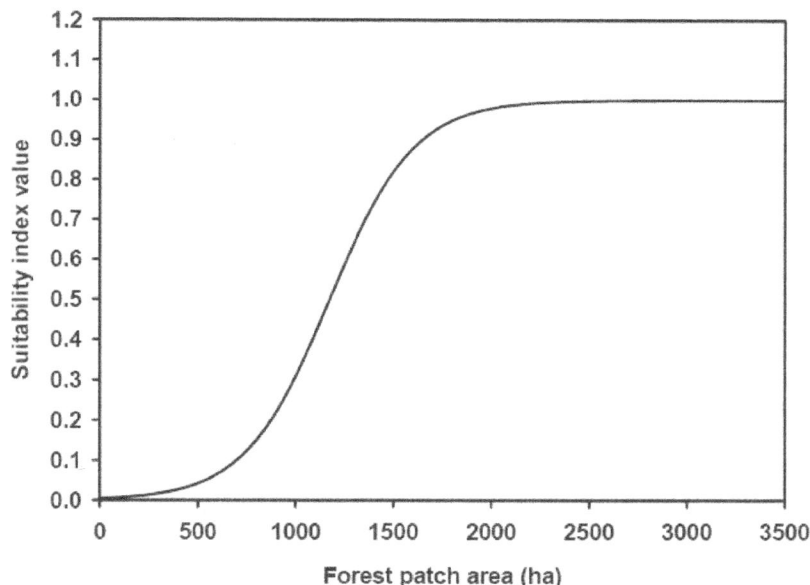

Figure 6.—Cerulean warbler habitat suitability for breeding as a function of deciduous forest area. Suitability value (SI_3) = 0.10 at 700 ha (min. area required for breeding, Robbins et al. 1989). Suitability value is maximum (= 1.00) for 3000 ha patches.

(minimum area required for breeding) (Robbins et al. 1989), and SI_3 = 1.00 for patches ≥3000 ha, and fit a sigmoid function:

$$SI_3 = \frac{1.0002}{\left(1 + e^{((- \, patchsize-1173\ 6472)/215\ 5805)}\right)}$$

The final habitat suitability value was the geometric mean of the three suitability indices:

$$HSI = \sqrt[3]{SI_1 \times SI_2 \times SI_3}$$

Application to test landscape

Suitability index 2, which assigned value based on tree age and ELT, contributed greatly to the heterogeneous pattern observed in the final habitat suitability map (Fig. 7). Stand size, homogeneity of tree age within a stand, as well as delineation of stand boundaries will influence the pattern observed when SI_2 is applied to other landscapes. Suitability index 3, which assigned value based on forest patch size, treated continuous canopy gaps (e.g., roads, power lines, and railroads) as patch boundaries. We considered the fact that the density or proportion of forested cells within a patch may affect patch value. For example, nonforested areas contained within large forested patches may reduce patch value. Conversely, predominantly forested landscapes that contain roads may be undervalued if roads create patches. Weakland and Wood (2002) found that cerulean warblers did not avoid internal edges (such as natural canopy gaps, open-canopy or partially open-canopy roads). Thus, we assumed patch size was an appropriate and conservative measure of forest value and did not include such effects in this model.

Henslow's Sparrow

Overview

The Henslow's sparrow is a short-distance, migratory bird that breeds in east-central North America and winters in the southeastern United States. Henslow's sparrows are a ground-nesting, obligate grassland species. Throughout their range the amount of habitat has declined from historic levels due to conversion of grasslands to intensive agricultural production, woody stem invasion (especially on abandoned agricultural lands), and fragmentation of remaining grasslands (Smith 1992). Henslow's sparrows are considered both area and edge sensitive, which may intensify the effects of habitat loss and fragmentation. Although no previous HSI model existed for Henslow's sparrows, several studies have described ecological relationships, including micro- and macro-habitat characteristics. We developed an HSI model based on reported ecological relationships and an extensive literature review. Primary sources for the literature review include Burhans (2002), Herkert et al. (2002), and references contained therein (e.g., Pruitt 1996).

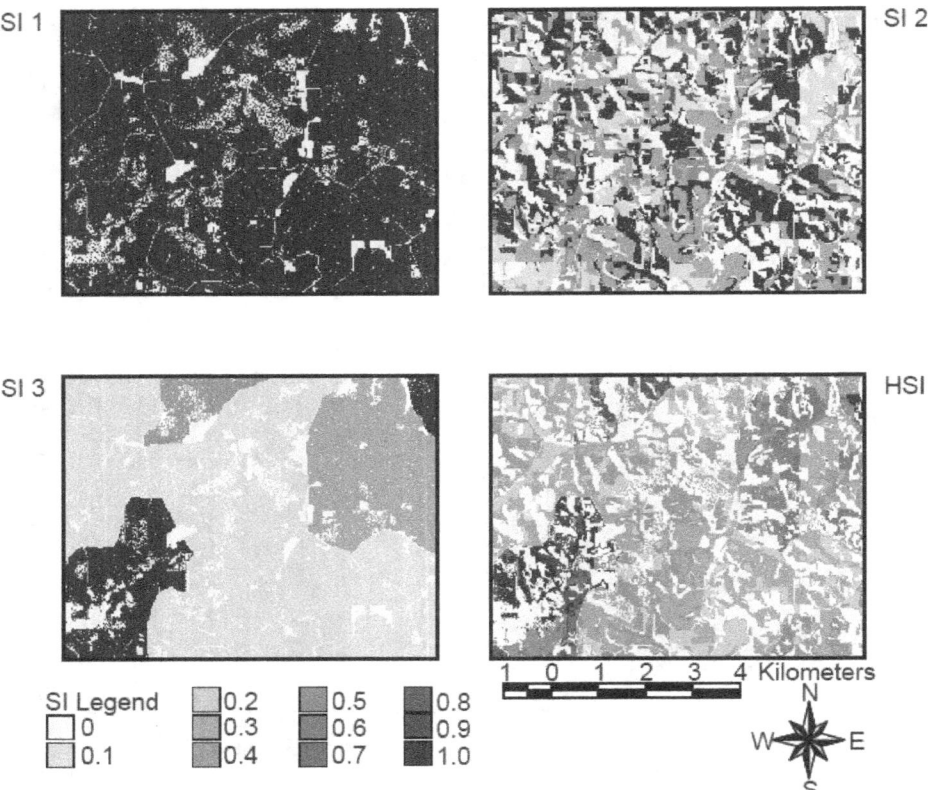

SI 1   SI 2

SI 3   HSI

SI Legend
0   0.2   0.5   0.8
0.1   0.3   0.6   0.9
       0.4   0.7   1.0

1 0 1 2 3 4 Kilometers

Figure 7.—Cerulean warbler habitat suitability for breeding on a 4,281-ha portion of the Hoosier National Forest, Indiana. The final habitat suitability value was the geometric mean of three suitability indices.

HSI model

We developed a Henslow's sparrow HSI model for breeding habitat in the Central Hardwoods Region. The HSI model contained three suitability indices that addressed land-cover type, area sensitivity, and edge sensitivity. The first suitability index (SI_1) identified grasslands as breeding habitat. Henslow's sparrows nest on the ground in grasslands, but are also found in hayfields, pastures, and meadows in the northeastern United States (Smith 1992). Both habitat structure and moisture are associated with Henslow's sparrow occupancy of grassland sites. Key structural characteristics include the presence of tall, dense grass with a well developed litter layer, standing dead vegetation, and little or no woody vegetation (Herkert et al. 2002). Henslow's sparrows may breed in fields that are infrequently mowed or lightly grazed (Skinner et al. 1984, Smith and Smith 1992, Cully and Michaels 2000), but frequent disturbance, such as burning, mowing, or haying, can render areas inhospitable (Pruitt 1996, Herkert 2001).

Henslow's sparrows breed principally in mesic grasslands (Hands et al. 1989), but also in dry and wet prairies (Swengel 1996). For SI_1 we assumed the disturbance interval on the Hoosier National Forest test landscape was sufficiently long for development of the necessary structural characteristics. Therefore, we evaluated only the land-cover type for each cell and set $SI_1 = 1.00$ if the land-cover type was grassland and $SI_1 = 0.00$ otherwise. The grassland cover type included warm and cool season grasslands, as well as hayfields, pastures, and prairies. Thus, the model may over-predict suitability in landscapes where Henslow's sparrows only use grasslands.

In the second suitability index (SI_2), we addressed a grassland area requirement. The minimum patch size used by Henslow's sparrows varies by region and also depends on landscape context. Samson (1980) and Harroff (1999) found Henslow's sparrows in grassland fragments as small as 10 ha, but we found no published accounts of sparrows in patches <10 ha (but see Mazur

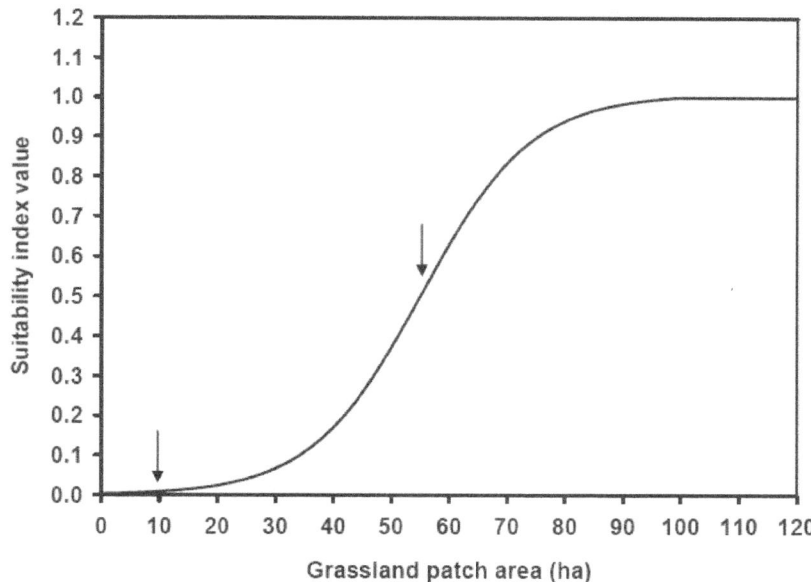

Figure 8.—Henslow's sparrow habitat suitability for breeding as a function of grassland area. Left arrow indicates 10 ha (minimum area requirement, Samson 1980, Harroff 1999) and right arrow indicates 55 ha (50 percent occurrence, Herkert 1994). Suitability value $(SI_2) = 0.00$ for patches ≤10 ha and $SI_2 = 1.00$ for patches >100 ha.

1996). In general, Henslow's sparrow density increases with increasing area (Winter and Faaborg 1999) and amount of grassland at the landscape level (Mazur 1996, McCoy 2000). We did not find published information to quantify a suitability relationship for the percentage of grassland at the landscape level. We refrained from subjectively assigning a landscape-level relationship and instead proceeded with a patch-level relationship. Herkert (1994) provided a quantitative estimate of the probability of occurrence based on area and estimated at least 55 ha are required to detect Henslow's sparrows 50 percent of the time. We plotted $SI_2 = 0.01$ for 10-ha patches, $SI_2 = 0.50$ for 55-ha patches, and $SI_2 = 1.00$ for 100-ha patches, and fit a sigmoid function (Fig. 8):

$$SI_2 = \frac{1.0090}{\left(1 + e^{(-1*(patchsize-55.1692)/9.5151))}\right)}$$

We applied this function to cells where $SI_1 > 0.00$ and patch size >10 ha. For grassland patches ≤10 ha, $SI_2 = 0.00$.

In the third suitability index (SI_3), we reduced the value of grassland habitat adjacent to forest and urban edges. Henlsow's sparrows nest in grasslands with little woody cover (Herkert 1994, Pruitt 1996) and do not nest within woody edges (Winter 1999). Henslow's sparrows exhibit both a demographic response (e.g., nest success) and a distributional response (e.g., density) to habitat edges. Nest success decreased with increased proximity to woody edges (Winter and Faaborg 1999, Winter et al. 2000), probably due to an increase in predator activity near woody edges (Winter et al. 2000). Adult density also decreased with increased proximity to edges (Winter et al. 2000, Bajema and Lima 2001). We found insufficient published information to develop a function describing the relationship between distance to edge and nest success or density because most studies used categorical data. Instead, we applied a moving window of 3 × 3 cells to pixels with a $SI_1 > 0.00$. The moving window assessed the land-cover type within the window and assigned $SI_3 = 0.00$ to the center pixel if the window contained non-grassland habitat. In this way, grassland immediately adjacent to edges received no suitability value. If the moving window contained only grassland habitat we assigned $SI_3 = 1.00$ to the center pixel. In other words, the center pixel retained the value assigned in SI_1 (= 1.00 for grassland).

The final habitat suitability value was the geometric mean of SI_1 and SI_2 multiplied by SI_3, to impose the edge-sensitivity penalty:

$$HSI = \left(\sqrt[2]{SI_1 \times SI_2}\right) \times SI_3$$

Application to test landscape

The first suitability index identified numerous patches of grassland; however, few patches exceeded the minimum

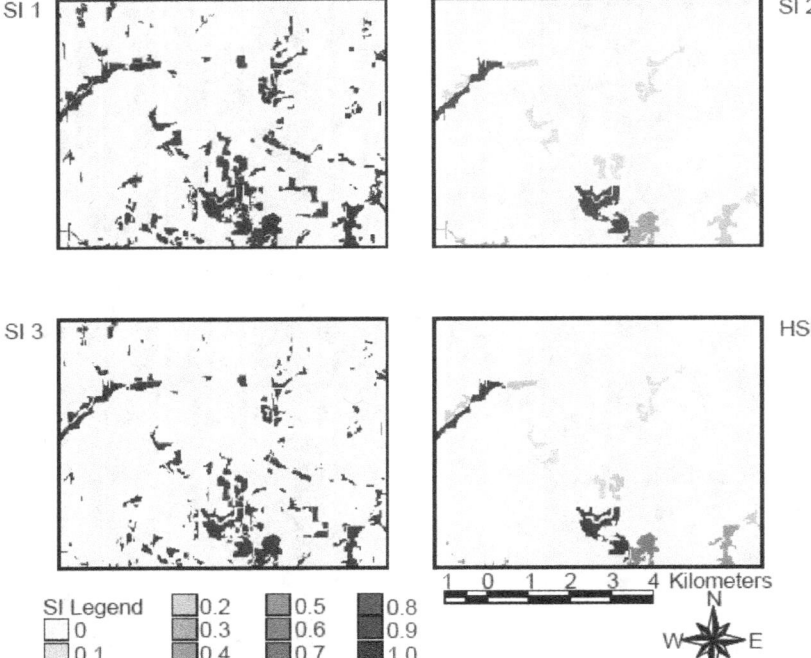

SI Legend
- 0
- 0.1
- 0.2
- 0.3
- 0.4
- 0.5
- 0.6
- 0.7
- 0.8
- 0.9
- 1.0

1 0 1 2 3 4 Kilometers

Figure 9.—Henslow's sparrow habitat suitability for breeding on a 4,281-ha portion of the Hoosier National Forest, Indiana.

patch size constraint of 10 ha (Fig. 9). Habitat suitability was greatest for large patches of grassland with minimal edge habitat.

Indiana Bat

Overview

The Indiana bat is a federally endangered, migratory species found in deciduous forests of the eastern United States. Indiana bats use different habitats for breeding and over-wintering. Indiana bats breed and raise their young in forested areas during the summer (Cope et al. 1974, Humphrey et al. 1977) and migrate to caves or abandoned mines to hibernate during the winter (Hall 1962).

HSI model

We developed an Indiana bat breeding season (summer) HSI model for the Central Hardwoods Region. Menzel et al. (2001) provided a review of available literature on habitat requirements for the Indiana bat, Rommé et al. (1995) developed a summer habitat HSI model, and Farmer et al. (2002) developed and evaluated an Indiana bat HSI. The Farmer et al. (2002) model contained suitability indexes for number of land-cover types, roost tree density, and percentage of landscape in forest. Of these, only roost tree density differed between sites with

and without Indiana bats. Our model differs from Farmer et al.'s model in two ways. First, we used Forest Inventory Analysis data and estimates of snag density by tree age class (Fan et al. 2003) to identify potential roost trees (SI_1), as recommended by Farmer et al. (2002). Second, we accounted for solar radiation of roost trees (SI_2 and SI_4). Finally, all of the SIs in our HSI model were based on reported ecological relationships for Indiana bats in the Central Hardwoods.

The first suitability index (SI_1) addressed maternity roost trees and was a function of snag suitability and density. Indiana bats form maternity roosts under the loose bark of live, dead, or dying trees (Kurta 1995) and in tree crevices (Kurta et al. 2002). Among living trees, roosts are most commonly found in shagbark hickory (Gardner et al. 1991, Callahan et al. 1997); however, the structural characteristics of snags may be more important than the tree species (Rommé et al. 1995). We derived a roost suitability function based on snag diameter at breast height (d.b.h.) and snag density as functions of tree age. Published estimates for the d.b.h. of roost trees used by maternity colonies range from 8-83 cm (Gardner et al. 1991), with an average d.b.h. of 35.0 cm (Carter et al. 2000), 36.7 cm (Gardner et al. 1991), 40.9 cm (Kurta et al. 1996), or 58.4 cm (Callahan et al. 1997). Based

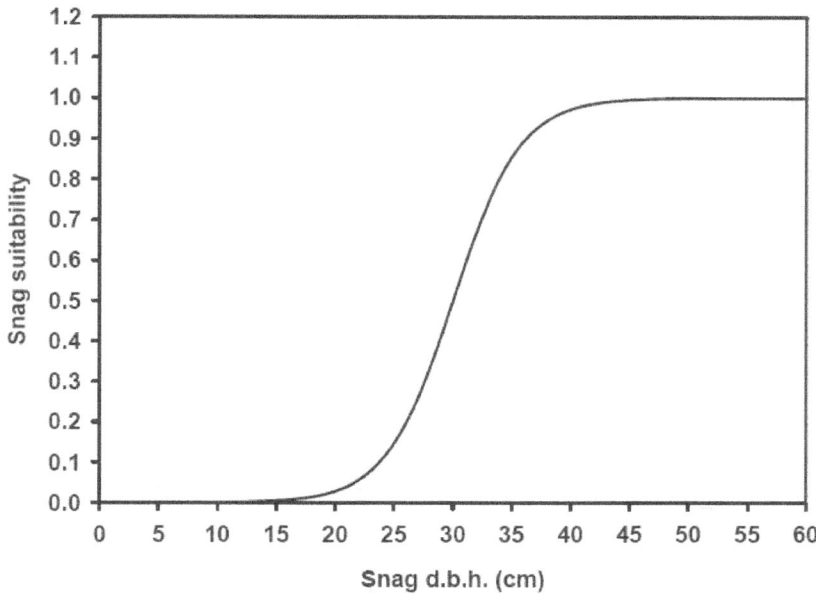

Figure 10.—Indiana bat "17–50" curve describing snag suitability as a function of diameter at breast height (cm).

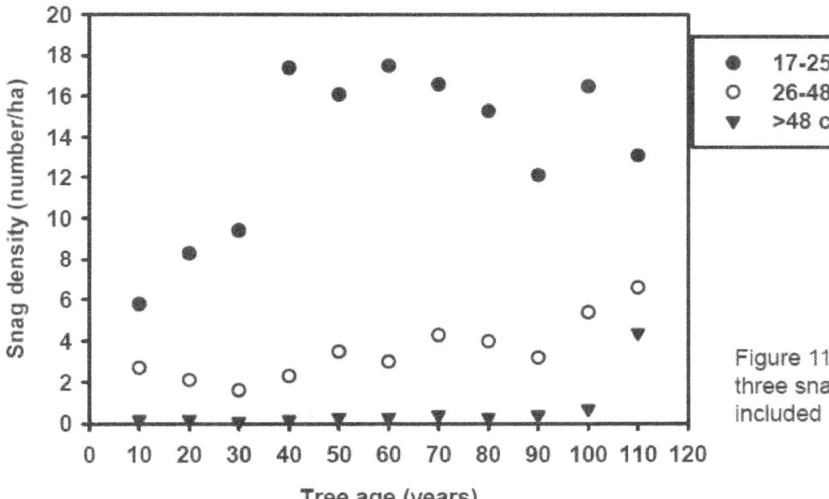

Figure 11.—Snag density by tree age class for three snag size classes. Age class 90 data was not included in analyses because of small sample size.

on published estimates and expert opinion[4], we assumed snags become suitable (SI = 0.01) at 17 cm d.b.h.; SI = 0.50 at 30 cm d.b.h.; and SI = 1.00 at 50 cm d.b.h. We fit a sigmoid function to the values with SigmaPlot (Indiana Bat "17-50" Curve, Fig. 10).

We used snag density (number of snags/ha) by size class information from Fan et al. (2003) to estimate snag density by tree age class (Fig. 11). Fan et al. (2003)

used data from remnant old-growth tracts and Forest Inventory Analysis data from Missouri to predict cavity tree and snag density as a function of rotation age. After consultation with Fan, we decided that the snag density information for age class 90 may be misrepresented due to low sample size and removed age class 90 data from the following analyses. We determined the average suitability by snag size class using the Indiana Bat "17-50" Curve (Fig. 10). We multiplied snag densities for each size class by the average suitability from the Indiana Bat "17-50" Curve and summed across each tree age class. We scaled the results to 0-1 by dividing each tree

[4]S. Amelon, Northern Research Station, U.S. Forest Service; and V. Brack, Jr., Environmental Solutions and Innovations, pers. comm.

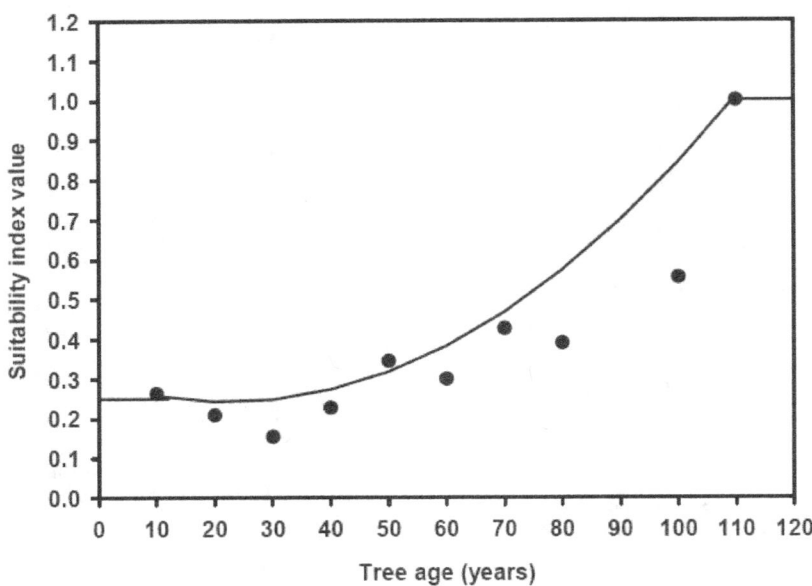

Figure 12.—Indiana bat habitat suitability for roost sites as a function of tree age, snag density, and size class.

age class value by the maximum value (age class 110) and plotted these relative values (Fig. 12). We fit a quadratic function for snag suitability by tree age class:

$$SI_1 = 0.2930 - 0.0045 \times age + 0.0001 \times age^2$$

and used this function to assign suitability value (SI_1) to trees 1-100 years of age. Suitability was maximum (SI_1 = 1.00) for trees ≥100 years of age.

In the second suitability index (SI_2), we identified open habitat and early successional forest. Indiana bats forage in open areas, including pastures and old fields (Brack 1983), over or near water (Jones et al. 1985, Gardner et al. 1996), and along borders of cropland (Clark et al. 1987a, 1987b) or habitat edges (Brack 1983). For SI_2 we assigned suitability value based on tree age: stands with trees 0-20 years of age, which included open areas, croplands, roads, and water as an artifact of our age-assignment process, received the highest suitability value (SI_2 = 1.00) and trees >20 years of age received SI_2 = 0.00.

In the third suitability index (SI_3), we constrained suitability of roost tree habitat by distance to water sources. Indiana bat maternity roosts are commonly located in riparian or bottomland areas (Gardner et al. 1991, Callahan et al. 1997), including wetlands (Kurta et al. 2002). In Indiana, Humphrey et al. (1977) found

two roost trees located less than 200 m from a creek that was used for foraging and Brack (1983) found a roost tree on the bank of a river. In Missouri, all reported colonies were found near a stream or river (Callahan et al. 1997). We assumed that all potential roost trees located within 1000 m of permanent water sources were accessible to Indiana bats and thus had maximum suitability (SI_3 = 1.00). We assigned suitability for potential roost trees located 1000-4000 m from water using the function (Fig. 13):

$$SI_3 = 1.33 - \sqrt[3]{\frac{dist}{1000}}$$

which declined linearly from SI_3 = 1.00 at 1000 m to SI_3 = 0.00 at 4000 m. Potential roost trees located more than 4000 m from a water source received SI_3 = 0.00.

In the fourth suitability index (SI_4), we evaluated roost exposure to solar radiation. Indiana bat maternity roosts often occur in trees exposed to direct sunlight (Humphrey et al. 1977, Kurta et al. 1993a, 1993b, Callahan et al. 1997). Solar radiation may decrease time of fetal development and increase juvenile growth (Callahan et al. 1997) or reduce metabolic costs for thermal regulation. Roost exposure to sunlight may result from gaps in forest canopy or may be due to roost location near a habitat edge. We used a 3 cell × 3 cell moving window to evaluate the interspersion of potential

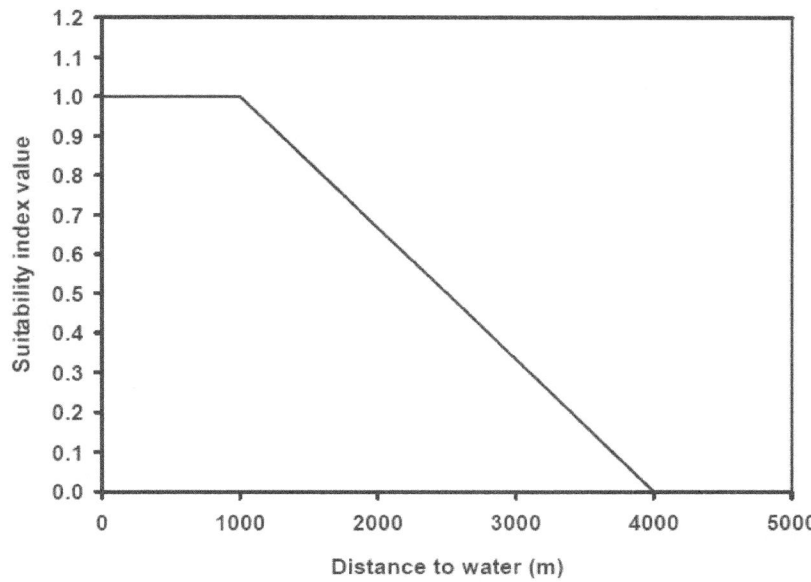

Figure 13.—Indiana bat habitat suitability for roost sites as a function of distance from roost tree to water. Suitability value (SI_3) = 1.00 for roost trees <1000 m from water and SI_3 = 0.00 for roost trees >4000 m from water.

roost trees (SI_1) with open areas and forest gaps (SI_2). If the center cell of the moving window had SI_1 >0.50 and any adjacent cell had SI_2 >0.50, then we assigned SI_4 = 1.00; otherwise we assigned SI_4 = 0.00. This procedure considered solar radiation from canopy gaps due to tree fall but did not account for canopy gaps created by large snags. Thus, it likely underestimated roost exposure to solar radiation.

The final habitat suitability value was the maximum of the composite roost site suitability or the foraging suitability:

$$HSI = Maximum\left[\left(\left(\sqrt{Maximum\left(SI_1, SI_2\right) \times SI_3}\right) \times SI_4\right),\right.$$
$$\left.\left(Maximum(SI_1, SI_2) \times SI_3 \times 0.5\right)\right]$$

Application to test landscape
This equation identified whether an individual cell contained a potential roost tree in forest (SI_1) or in open/early successional habitat adjacent to forest (SI_2), and then considered the value of that cell based on the potential for solar radiation (SI_4) and distance to water (SI_3) (Fig. 14). If a cell did not have value as a potential roost site (SI_1) or as an open area for foraging (SI_2), it still had value as foraging habitat or alternative (secondary) roost sites. Thus, the remainder of the equation captured the value of forests for foraging habitat and alternative roost sites (SI_1), or the value of open areas for

foraging habitat (SI_2), modified by the distance to water. Distance to water was not limiting in the test landscape and therefore SI_3 = 1.00. The final HSI map contained large areas of forest that may be used for foraging and alternative roost sites. The greatest potential for primary roost sites was along forest edges.

Northern Bobwhite
Overview
The northern bobwhite is a nonmigratory game species that breeds throughout the eastern United States. In the northern part of their range, bobwhite are associated with heterogeneous, patchy landscapes that contain early successional woody cover, grasslands, and row crops (Roseberry and Sudkamp 1998). Due to their importance as a game species, northern bobwhite are a popular research species, perhaps the most intensively studied bird in the world (Guthery 1997). Several HSI (or HSI-type) models exist for northern bobwhite, including an early quantitative method for evaluating habitat from aerial photos (Backs 1981), the original HSI developed by Schroeder (1985), and several recent models that incorporate landscape-level attributes (e.g., Brady et al. 1993, Roseberry 1993, Roseberry and Sudkamp 1998, Burger et al. 2004).

HSI model
We developed a northern bobwhite HSI model for the Central Hardwoods Region. The first suitability

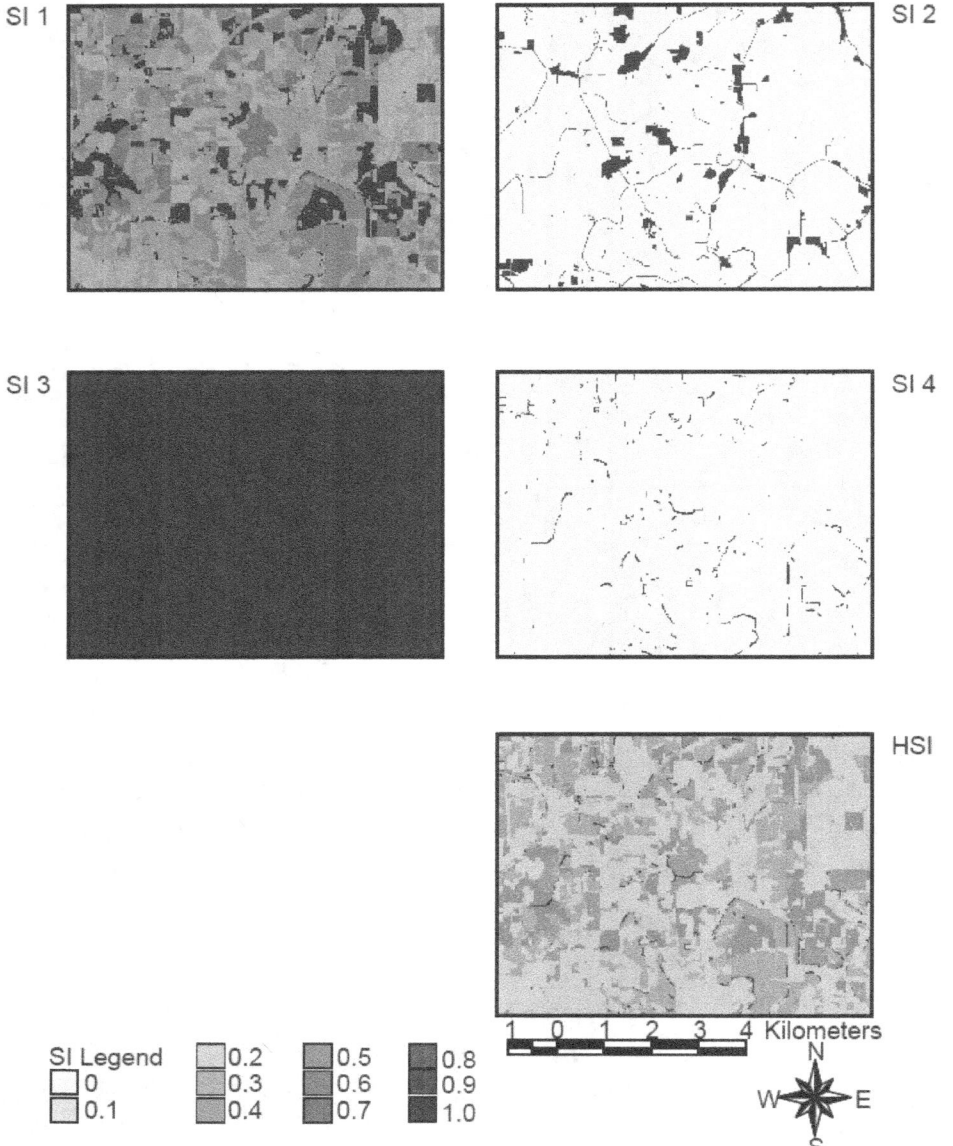

SI Legend
☐ 0
☐ 0.1
☐ 0.2
☐ 0.3
☐ 0.4
☐ 0.5
☐ 0.6
☐ 0.7
☐ 0.8
☐ 0.9
☐ 1.0

Figure 14.—Indiana bat habitat suitability for a 4,281-ha portion of the Hoosier National Forest, Indiana.

index (SI_1) identified grasslands used for nest sites, cover, and food. Northern bobwhite nest in fields where plant succession has progressed at least 1 year following disturbance (Dimmick 1972). Prescribed fire or mechanical disturbance conducted every 1-5 years maintains habitat conditions for bobwhite populations (Stoddard 1931, Landers and Mueller 1986). We evaluated the land-cover type for each cell and set SI_1 = 0.50 if the land-cover type was grassland and SI_1 = 0.00 otherwise.

In the second suitability index (SI_2), we identified food sources. Bobwhite eat seeds of agricultural crops and weeds, as well as forest, agricultural, and rangeland vegetation, especially understory plants and plants along field margins (Brennan 1999). Common foods include beggarweeds (*Bidens* spp.), ragweeds (*Ambrosia* spp.), *Lespedezas* spp., corn (*Zea* spp.), partridge peas (*Chamaecrista* spp.), acorns (*Quercus* spp.), sumacs (*Rhus* spp.), pine seeds (*Pinus* spp.), soybeans (*Glycine* spp.), and rowpeas (*Pisum* spp.) (Landers and Johnson 1976).

Seeds from agricultural crops, such as corn, soybeans, and wheat (*Triticum* spp.), predominate fall and winter diets (Larimer 1960, Roseberry and Klimstra 1984). We assumed grasslands identified in SI_1 provided food in addition to nesting habitat and that woody edges identified in SI_3 provided food in addition to escape cover. Therefore, we used SI_2 to identify agricultural food sources. We evaluated the land-cover type for each cell and set $SI_2 = 0.40$ if the land-cover type was cropland and $SI_2 = 0.00$ otherwise.

In the third suitability index (SI_3), we identified woody edge cover. Bobwhite prefer areas where approximately 50 percent of the ground is exposed and 50 percent contains upright growth of herbaceous and woody vegetation (Schroeder 1985). Brushy or woody edges along crop fields and grasslands often meet these requirements. In addition to grasslands and croplands, bobwhite will also use open canopy (<50 percent) pinelands and mixed pine-hardwood forests (DeVos and Mueller 1993, Brennan 1999). A landscape-level assessment of bobwhite habitat suitability in Illinois associated bobwhite abundance with high woody edge density (≥30 m/ha) (Roseberry and Sudkamp 1998). Woody edge often is used for escape cover (Williams et al. 2000), thus the first 30 m of woody cover from a field edge appears the most important, with use declining with distance from the field edge. We used a 60-m moving window to identify forest within 30 m of grassland or cropland. If the center pixel contained forest ≥1 year of age and the remaining cells contained either grassland or cropland, we set $SI_3 = 0.30$ for the center pixel. Otherwise, we set $SI_3 = 0.00$.

In the fourth suitability index (SI_4), we used a moving window to evaluate interspersion of habitat types. In agricultural regions, the interspersion of nesting (grassland), food (grassland and cropland), and cover (woody edge) provide optimum habitat for bobwhite (Roseberry and Sudkamp 1998). The proportion of each habitat type varies somewhat by study: 30-65 percent row crops and 15-30 percent grassland in Illinois (Roseberry and Sudkamp 1998); 75-90 percent open land consisting of 50-60 percent cropland and 20-30 percent grassland in Missouri (Dailey 1989);

and 30-40 percent grassland, 40-60 percent cropland, 5-20 percent brushy cover, and 5-40 percent woodland cover (Johnsgard 1973). We evaluated the proportion of grassland, cropland, and woody edge using a moving window with a 360-m radius. The area within the moving window equaled 40.7 ha, which approximated the maximum average northern bobwhite home range of 38 ha[5] reported within the Central Hardwoods. Estimates of bobwhite home range size vary by season and location. Home ranges averaged 38 ha in winter in northeast Missouri[5], 9 ha (range 6-11 ha) during a late-winter period with prolonged snow cover in southern Illinois (Roseberry 1964), and 15 ha (range 12-19 ha) for late winter in a different year in Illinois (Bartholomew 1967). We based the ideal proportion on the midpoints of Roseberry and Sudkamp (1998): grassland = 0.22, cropland = 0.47, and woody cover = 0.31, and set $SI_4 = 0.50$ if the window contained the ideal proportion. The suitability value declined toward zero as a function of the difference between the observed proportion within the moving window and the ideal proportion:

$$SI_4 = 0.5 * ((1 - PROP1) * (1 - PROP2) * (1 - PROP3))$$

where *PROP*1, *PROP*2, and *PROP*3 equaled the absolute value of the observed proportion minus the ideal proportion of grassland, cropland, and woody cover, respectively. In other words, SI_4 was maximized when the observed proportions equaled the ideal proportions.

We used the fifth suitability index (SI_5) to zero out roads and urban areas that received suitability value from SI_4 because we assigned value to all cells based on the composition of habitat within the moving window. We assigned $SI_5 = 1.00$ for forest, cropland, and grassland, otherwise $SI_5 = 0.00$.

The final habitat suitability value was the sum of 1) the maximum value of SI_1, SI_2, and SI_3; and 2) the product of SI_4 and SI_5 (Fig. 15):

$$HSI = Maximum(Maximum(SI_1, SI_2), SI_3) + (SI_4 \times SI_5)$$

---

[5]Burger, L.W., Jr., Mississippi State University, pers. comm.

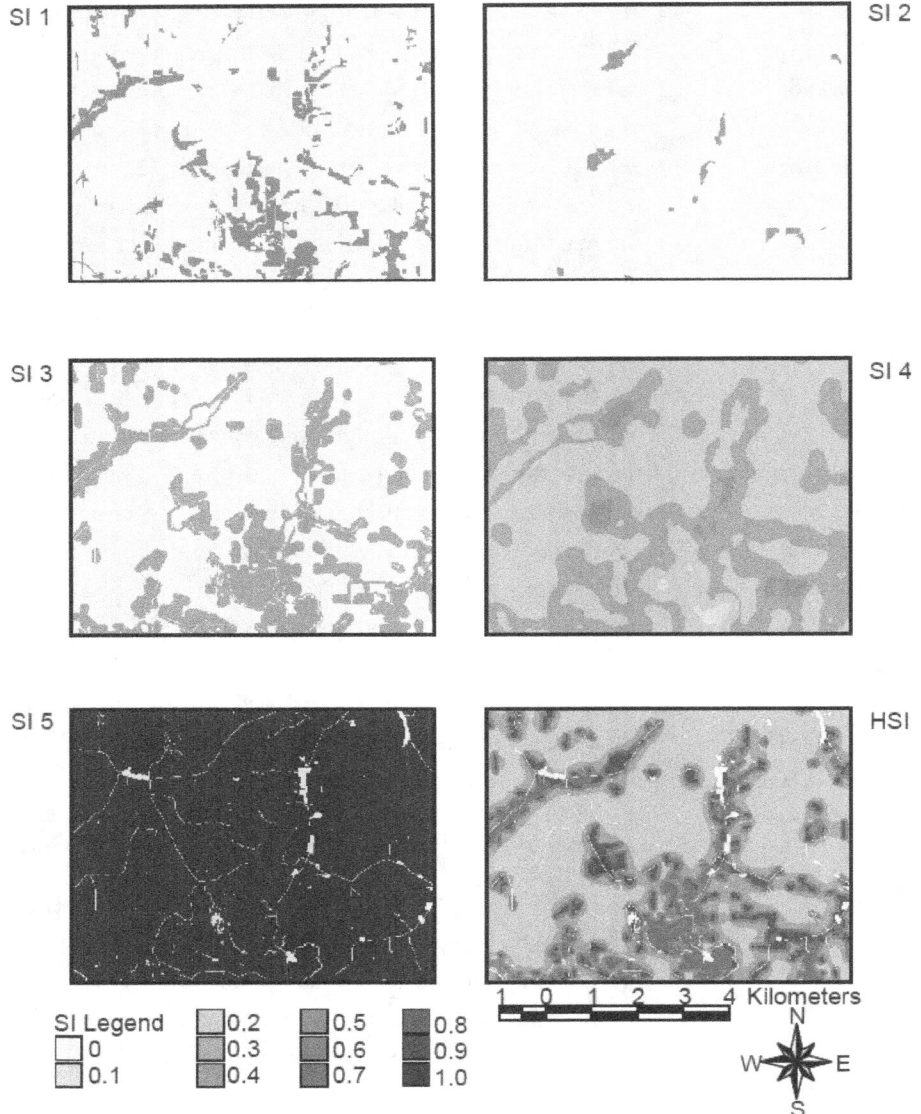

Figure 15.—Northern bobwhite habitat suitability for a 4,281-ha portion of the Hoosier National Forest, Indiana.

We used an additive HSI equation as opposed to a multiplicative equation because we recognized that grassland, cropland, or woody cover provided bobwhite habitat; however, the highest suitability value occurred when at least two of the three habitat types were present within the moving window.

Application to test landscape

The first, second, and third suitability indices identified grasslands, croplands, and woody edges within the landscape. The fourth suitability index identified several areas where the interspersion of these three habitat requirements occurred. After excluding nonusable open areas (i.e., roads and urban areas), the final HSI map reflected the cumulative value of each habitat type and its interspersion. In general, grasslands adjacent to woody edges provided the greatest area of suitable habitat on the landscape.

Ruffed Grouse

Overview

The ruffed grouse (*Bonasa umbellus*) is a nonmigratory game species that breeds throughout the boreal forests of North America and in portions of deciduous forest in the eastern United States. Ruffed grouse are associated with early successional forests in all parts of their range, including aspen and poplar forests in the north and oak-hickory or mixed deciduous-coniferous forests in the south and east (Rusch et al. 2000). Cade and Sousa (1985) developed the first HSI model for grouse; however, the model relied on aspen buds for winter food and thus has limited application within the Central Hardwoods due to the low abundance of aspen.

HSI model

We developed a ruffed grouse HSI model for the Central Hardwoods Region. The first suitability index (SI_1) identified potential food sources for ruffed grouse. Ruffed grouse diets vary seasonally but usually contain leaves, buds, and fruits of deciduous forest plants (Rusch et al. 2000). During brood rearing, adults and chicks eat invertebrates (Bump et al. 1947) in addition to the leaves of herbaceous plants (Norman and Kirkpatrick 1984). In late autumn and winter, hard mast, consisting primarily of white oak, red oak, chinkapin oak, and black oak acorns, are an important food source (Thompson and Fritzell 1986). We assumed hard mast was the most limiting of these food sources given its predominance in fall and winter diets and used SI_1 to estimate suitability based on acorn mast production. Sullivan (2001) developed models for acorn production based on tree age, species (white oak or red oak) and ELT, which he subsequently modified[6] for application to the Hoosier National Forest.

In the second suitability index (SI_2), we identified early successional forest used for nesting, feeding, and roosting. While ruffed grouse in the northern portion of their range are associated with aspen-dominated forests (Gullion et al. 1962, Kubisiak et al. 1980, DeStefano and Rusch 1984, Kubisiak 1984), grouse in the southern portion of their range use early successional forests containing oaks, hickories, and pines (Rodgers 1980, Gudlin and Dimmick 1984, Hunyadi 1984, Wiggers et al. 1992). Grouse also will use young cedar stands for winter roosts (Thompson and Fritzell 1988). For SI_2 we assigned suitability value based on tree age and ELT. Stands with trees 1-20 years of age on mesic ridges, slopes, and bottomlands received the highest suitability

---

[6]N. Sullivan, Northern Research Station, U.S. Forest Service, pers. comm.

value (SI_2 = 1.00). Stands with trees 1-20 years of age located on dry ridges and slopes had SI_2 = 0.80. For both mesic and dry sites, suitability value declined to zero with increasing stand age.

In the third suitability index (SI_3), we addressed known early successional forest area requirements. Grouse home ranges vary in size depending on region and forest type. In central Pennsylvania, male home ranges averaged 5.0-9.4 ha in the breeding season and 11.0-14.0 ha in the summer (McDonald et al. 1998). Home ranges of male grouse in Missouri ranged from 45-68 ha in spring and summer to 84-109 ha in fall and winter (Thompson and Fritzell 1989). In southern Illinois, grouse home ranges were 26.9-226.2 ha (Woolf et al. 1984). We assumed the minimum year-round early successional forest area requirement was 4 ha; however, patches smaller than 4 ha may be used or defended during the spring (Archibald 1975, Maxson 1989). Therefore, we developed a suitability function to assign value to patches 0.01-4 ha:

$$SI_3 = patchsize / 4$$

where $patchsize$ was the area of early successional forest. Patches of early successional forest >4 ha received maximum suitability value (SI_3 = 1.00).

In the fourth suitability index (SI_4), we used a moving window with a 180-m radius to evaluate the interspersion of early successional forest and acorn production. The 10-ha area of the moving window corresponded to the average home-range size of ruffed grouse (McDonald et al. 1998). We calculated SI_4 in three steps. First we assigned a value (M_4) based on the proportion of acorn mast within the moving window. We plotted M_4 = 0.01 for proportion of mast = 0.00, M_4 = 0.50 at 0.05, and M_4 = 1.00 at 0.10, and fit a sigmoid function to these values:

$$M_4 = \frac{0.999478}{\left(1 + e^{((-ppnMast - 0.0499892)/0.00288211)}\right)}$$

If the proportion of mast exceeded 0.10, the mast value was M_4 = 1.00. Second, we assigned a value (ES_4) based on the proportion of early successional forest that met the minimum area requirement within the moving window. We plotted ES_4 = 0.01 for proportion of early

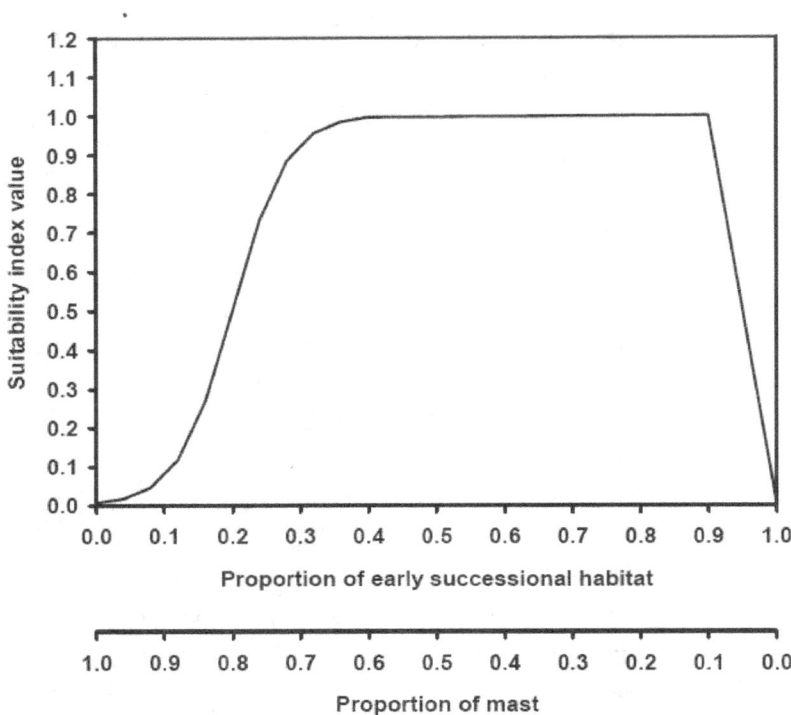

Figure 16.—Ruffed grouse habitat suitability as a function of early successional habitat and proportion of mast within a 10-ha moving window.

succesional forest = 0.00, ES_4 = 0.50 at 0.20, and ES_4 = 1.00 at 0.40, and fit a sigmoid function to these values:

$$ES_4 = \frac{1.00329}{\left(1 + e^{((-ppnES - 0.200233)/0.0398903)}\right)}$$

If the proportion of early successional forest exceeded 0.40, ES_4 = 1.00. Last, we calculated the suitability value as the product of the mast value and the early successional forest value (Fig. 16):

$$SI_4 = M_4 \times ES_4$$

In SI_1 we assumed that acorn mast was an important food source for grouse during late fall and winter (Thompson and Fritzell 1986). When applied to SI_4, this assumption will produce SI_4 = 0.00 when M_4 = 0.00. The proportion of mast within the moving window may equal zero when the proportion of early successional forest within the moving window is 1.00 (e.g., the size of an early successional forest patch exceeds the size of the moving window). Future users may want to adjust the function for M_4 such that M_4 receives a nonzero value (i.e., $\geq$ 0.01) to retain early successional patches in the SI_4 equation.

In the fifth suitability value (SI_5), we addressed a minimum forest area requirement. Although grouse use relatively small patches of early successional forest, these patches must be imbedded within a larger, contiguous forested area. In Missouri, grouse were released in early successional patches located within forests of 109, 259, and 1090 ha (Hunyadi 1984). Backs (1984) recommended that release locations in Indiana have a minimum of 400 ha of relatively contiguous forested area surrounded by 5-8 km² of primarily forested cover types. We plotted SI_5 = 0.01 for forested area = 100 ha, SI_5 = 0.25 at 200 ha, and SI_5 = 1.00 at 400 ha, and fit a sigmoid function to these values (Fig. 17):

$$SI_5 = \frac{1.0009}{\left(1 + e^{((-patchsize - 277.118)/24.6569)}\right)}$$

The suitability value increased to a maximum of SI_5 = 1.00 for patches $\geq$400 ha.

The final habitat suitability value was the geometric mean of 1) the maximum value of SI_1 or the geometric mean of SI_2 and SI_3; and 2) SI_4; multiplied by SI_5 (Fig. 18):

$$HSI = \left(\sqrt{Maximum\left(SI_1, \sqrt{SI_2 \times SI_3}\right) \times SI_4}\right) \times SI_5$$

Suitability index value
1.2
1.1
1.0
0.9
0.8
0.7
0.6
0.5
0.4
0.3
0.2
0.1
0.0
0
100
200
300
400
500
Forest area (ha)

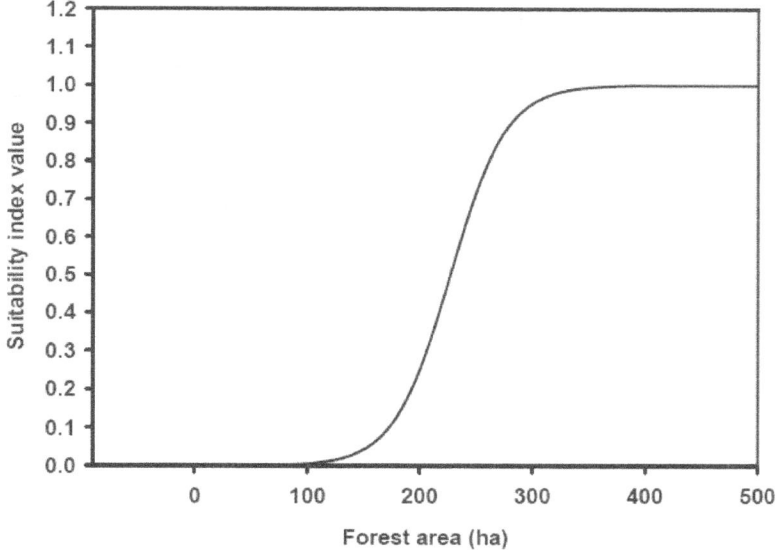

Figure 17.—Ruffed grouse habitat suitability as a function of forest area. Suitability value (SI_5) = 0.00 for patches ≤100 ha and SI_5 = 1.00 for patches >400 ha.

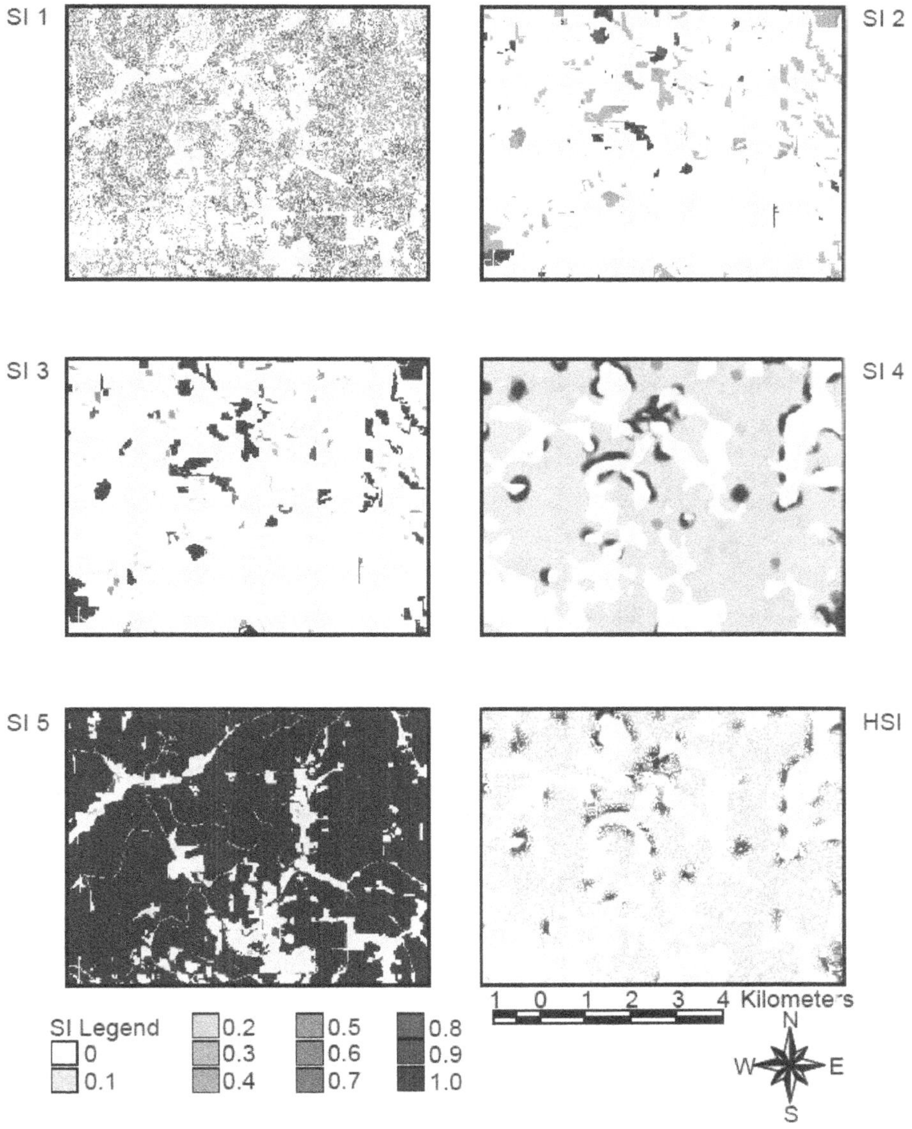

SI 1
SI 2
SI 3
SI 4
SI 5
HSI
SI Legend
0
0.1
0.2
0.3
0.4
0.5
0.6
0.7
0.8
0.9
1.0
1 0 1 2 3 4 Kilometers
N
W
E
S

Figure 18.—Ruffed grouse habitat suitability for a 4,281-ha portion of the Hoosier National Forest, Indiana.

Application to test landscape

We used the maximum of either acorn mast production (SI_1) or early successional forest patches $\left(\sqrt{SI_2 \times SI_3} \right)$ because a single cell cannot provide both habitat requirements. The fourth suitability index identified several areas where the interspersion of acorn mast production and early successional forest patches occurred. After imposing the minimum forested area constraint (SI_5), the final HSI map consisted of several small patches of suitable grouse habitat (e.g., early successional forest embedded within mast-producing forest) surrounded by predominantly unsuitable habitat.

Timber Rattlesnake

Overview

The timber rattlesnake is the only woodland rattlesnake in the eastern United States. During the active season (May–September) typical habitat includes rocky, open sites in deciduous hardwood forest (Klauber 1997) and lightly wooded clearings and oak-hickory knolls containing boulders, rock slabs, and outcrop fissures (Brown 1992). Reinert (1984a) found timber rattlesnakes in forested areas with greater surface vegetation and less rock density than in other portions of their range. Because rattlesnakes hibernate for up to 7 months of the year in southern Indiana (Walker 2000), over-wintering sites (hibernacula) are critical habitat features. We developed our HSI model based on the reported ecological relationships from studies conducted in Indiana (Walker 2000), Pennsylvania (Reinert 1984a, 1984b), New York (Brown et al. 1982, Brown 1991), New Jersey (Reinert and Zappalorti 1988), South Carolina (Andrews and Gibbons 2005), and West Virginia (Adams 2005).

HSI model

We developed a timber rattlesnake HSI model for breeding habitat in the Central Hardwoods Region. The first suitability index (SI_1) identified early successional forested habitat used for foraging and basking. Rattlesnakes eat a variety of animals but the primary prey species are small mammals. Early successional habitat, such as canopy gaps and forest edges, affects small mammal abundance (Osbourne et al. 2005), diversity, and richness (Sekgororoane and Dilworth

1995). Additionally, canopy gaps may provide rattlesnake rookery (i.e., birthing) and basking opportunities (Adams 2005). While rattlesnakes are typically found in forests with large coarse woody debris (e.g., fallen logs) and high canopy closure, most rattlesnake relocations in southern Indiana were associated with small canopy breaks where sunlight reached the ground (Walker 2000). Gravid females were particularly associated with forest clearings in Indiana (Gibson and Kingsbury 2002) and with road edges, log landings, and regenerating hardwood stands in West Virginia (Adams 2005).

We grouped ELTs to account for the influence of moisture on vegetation growth. Mesic ridges, north and east slopes, and bottomlands constituted the mesic ELTs, and dry ridges and south and west slopes the dry ELTs. We assigned $SI_1 = 1.00$ to stands 1–10 years of age on both mesic and dry ELTs. Mesic sites with stands >10 years of age had $SI_1 = 0.00$, but stands on dry sites retained higher suitability value due to delayed canopy closure. We assigned $SI_1 = 0.50$ for stands 11–20 years of age, $SI_1 = 0.30$ for stands 21–30 years of age, and $SI_1 = 0.10$ for stands 31–40 years of age. Dry ELTs with trees >40 years of age had $SI_1 = 0.00$.

In the second suitability index (SI_2), we identified woody debris habitat used for cover and foraging. Rattlesnakes use mid- to late-successional second growth deciduous forest with 62 percent mean canopy closure and 19.3 cm mean d.b.h. (Reinert 1984a). Males use predominantly forest sites (69 percent canopy cover) with moderate to dense forest floor vegetation (Reinert 1984b). Nongravid females used forested sites with 67 percent mean canopy cover but with less surface vegetation than male sites (Reinert 1984b). We assumed stands containing trees >100 years of age contained coarse woody debris suitable for rattlesnake use, and that suitability declined with decreasing stand age. We evaluated tree age for each cell and set $SI_2 = 0.00$ for trees 1–30 years of age. For trees 31–100 years of age, we assigned suitability using the function (Fig. 19):

$$SI_2 = \frac{treeage}{70} - 0.42857$$

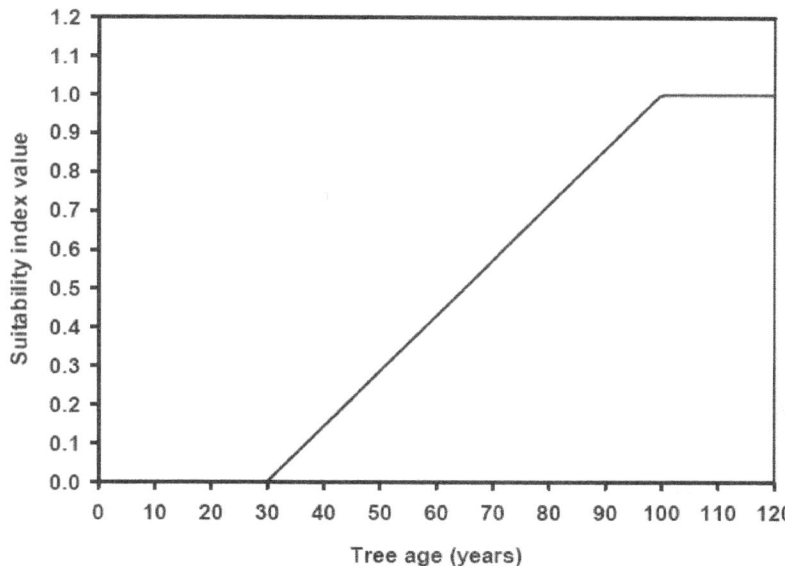

Figure 19.—Timber rattlesnake habitat suitability as a function of stand age. Suitability value (SI_2) = 0.00 for stands ≤30 years and SI_2 = 1.00 for stands >100 years.

We developed this equation by fitting a linear regression equation such that SI_2 = 0.00 at 30 years of age and SI_2 = 1.00 for trees ≥100 years of age.

In the third suitability index (SI_3), we evaluated the proportion of woody debris and foraging habitat using a moving window with an 850-m radius. The area within the moving window equaled 227 ha, which approximated the maximum average male rattlesnake home range size of 207 ha (Reinert and Zappalorti 1988). Home range sizes in southern Indiana averaged 174 ha (range 112-382 ha) for males and 72 ha (range 15-181 ha) for females (Walker 2000). We based the ideal proportion for foraging and woody debris cover on the average percentage canopy cover of rattlesnake locations reported by Walker (2000): foraging, basking, and rookery (open canopy) = 0.15, and woody debris cover and foraging (closed canopy) = 0.85. We set SI_3 = 1.00 if the window contained the ideal proportion. The suitability value declined toward zero with increasing difference between the actual proportion within the moving window and the ideal proportion.

In the fourth suitability index (SI_4), we assigned value based on proximity to den sites or hibernacula. Rattlesnake habitat requirements vary by sex and reproductive status. Gravid female rattlesnakes often bask on rocks near den sites (Reinert 1984b). The mean dispersal distance for female rattlesnakes (gravid and nongravid) in New York averaged 280 m and ranged from 191-425 m (Brown et al. 1982). In West Virginia the mean dispersal distance was 584 m (range 328-832 m) for gravid females and 872 m (range 618-1121 m) for nongravid females (Adams 2005). The spatial requirements for male rattlesnakes greatly exceed the requirements for nongravid females. Male rattlesnakes dispersed up to 1.4 km from hibernacula in New York (Brown et al. 1982) and up to 3.6 km in West Virginia (Adams 2005). Male rattlesnakes also make movements during the breeding season of 2 km (Walker 2000). Based on the large spatial requirements of rattlesnakes in New York, Brown (1993) estimated a population with 50 adults would require a 2.4 km radius of protected land around a den site. We calculated the distance from each cell to the nearest den site and assigned SI_4 = 1.00 to cells within 500 m of den sites. For cells located 500-2500 m from den sites, we assigned suitability using the function (Fig. 20):

$$SI_4 = 1.25 - 0.0005 \times distden$$

where *distden* is the distance from a cell to the nearest den site. Suitability declined with increasing distance from a den site. Cells located >2500 m from a den site received SI_4 = 0.00. This suitability index will underestimate the suitability of habitat in situations where not all den site locations are known. Therefore, comprehensive knowledge of den site locations is needed. We recommend consulting with local experts to identify den sites.

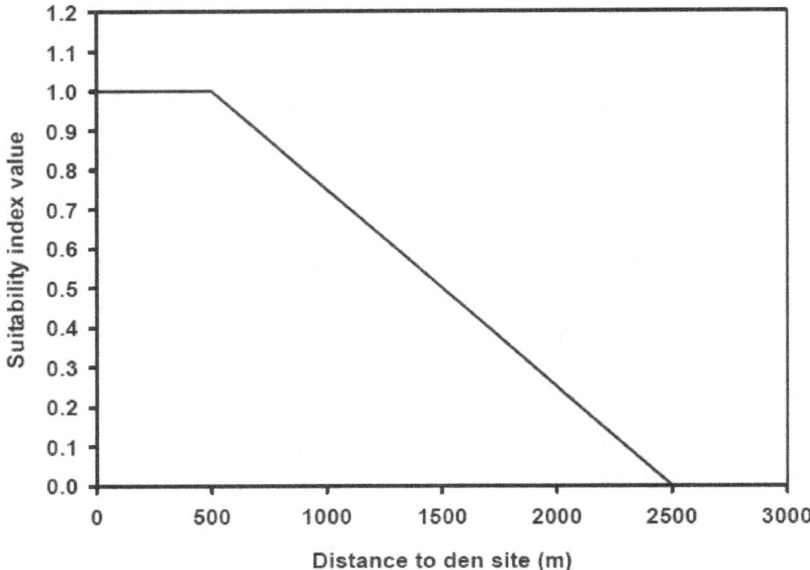

Figure 20.—Timber rattlesnake habitat suitability as a function of distance from den sites. Suitability value (SI_4) = 1.00 for habitat ≤500m from den sites and SI_4 = 0.00 for habitat >2500m from den sites.

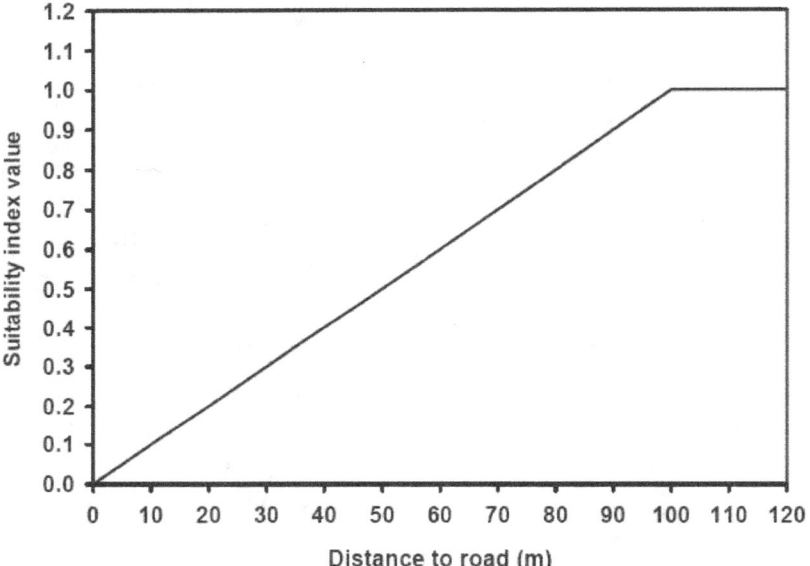

Figure 21.—Timber rattlesnake habitat suitability as a function of distance from roads.

In the fifth suitability index (SI_5), we reduced the suitability value of habitat near roads. Roads may present barriers to rattlesnake movements (Fitch 1999, Sealy 2002) or reduce rattlesnake survival (Seigel and Pilgrim 2002). An experimental study on the Savannah River Site in South Carolina revealed that large rattlesnakes had a greater tendency to avoid roads than smaller rattlesnakes (Andrews and Gibbons 2005). Male rattlesnakes had higher road mortality during the breeding season than females, presumably due to increased movements associated with mate searching (Aldridge and Brown 1995). We calculated the distance from each cell to the nearest road and assigned SI_5 = 1.00 to cells greater than 100 m from roads. For cells <100 m from roads we assigned suitability using the function (Fig. 21):

$$SI_5 = \frac{distroad}{100}$$

where *distroad* is the distance from a cell to the nearest road. Suitability increased with increasing distance from a road.

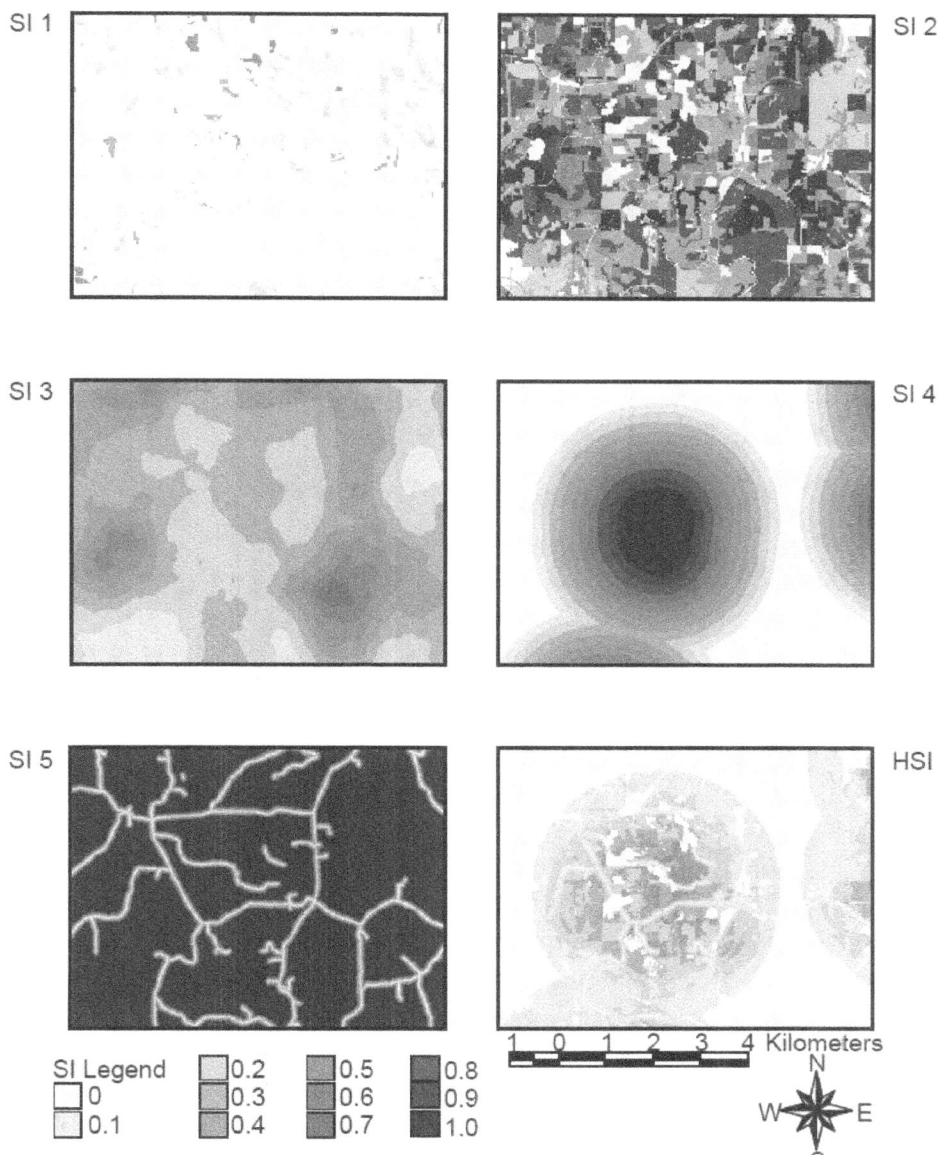

SI 1

SI 2

SI 3

SI 4

SI 5

HSI

SI Legend
0
0.1
0.2
0.3
0.4
0.5
0.6
0.7
0.8
0.9
1.0

1 0 1 2 3 4 Kilometers

N W E S

Figure 22.—Timber rattlesnake habitat suitability for a 4,281-ha portion of the Hoosier National Forest, Indiana.

The final habitat suitability value was the geometric mean of the maximum value of SI_1 or SI_2 multiplied by SI_3, and reduced by the product of SI_4 and SI_5 (Fig. 22):

$$HSI = \left(\sqrt{Maximum(SI_1, SI_2) \times SI_3} \right) \times SI_4 \times SI_5$$

Application to test landscape

We used the maximum of either the first or the second suitability indices because a single cell could not contain both early successional and mid- to late-successional habitat. We reduced the value of each cell based on its distance from den sites and roads. These two requirements greatly reduced the amount of suitable habitat; the final HSI map reflects the importance of conserving near-den habitat for rattlesnakes. We used pseudo-den locations in the test landscape to demonstrate the full capability of the model without revealing actual den locations.

Wood Thrush

Overview

The wood thrush (*Hylocichla mustelina*) is a neotropical migratory bird that breeds in eastern North America and winters in Central America. Wood thrushes nest in

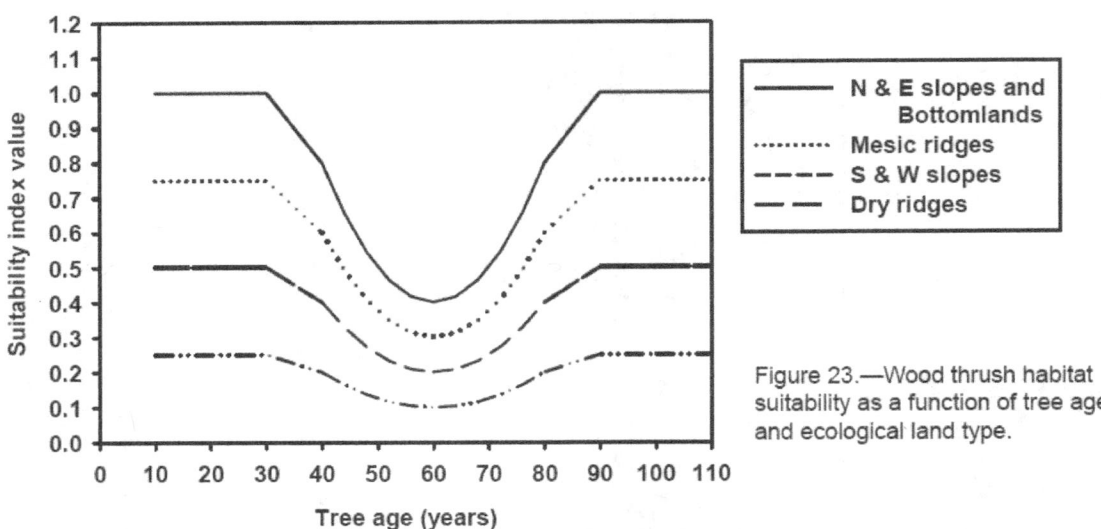

Figure 23.—Wood thrush habitat suitability as a function of tree age and ecological land type.

shrubs and small trees of deciduous, mixed-deciduous coniferous, bottomland hardwood, and pine forests with deciduous understory (Roth et al. 1996). Existing habitat studies for wood thrush indicate forest area (Robbins et al. 1989), harvest type and age (Thompson et al. 1992, Robinson and Robinson 1999, Pagen et al. 2000, Gram et al. 2003), as well as canopy height, tree density, and type of canopy cover (e.g., deciduous vs. coniferous) (Robbins et al. 1989), are important habitat features. A breeding habitat suitability index model for the Gulf of Maine watershed used vegetative cover, forest patch size, distance from edge, and moisture regime as suitability indices (Banner and Schaller 2001).

HSI model

We developed a wood thrush HSI model for breeding habitat in the Central Hardwoods Region. The first suitability index (SI_1) identified suitable tree species for nesting habitat. Wood thrush nest in a variety of deciduous trees, and conifer stands are used if a deciduous subcanopy is present (Roth et al. 1996). We accomplished this by evaluating the dominant tree type for each cell and setting SI_1 = 0.20 if the dominant tree type was pine or cedar, and SI_1 = 1.00 otherwise.

In the second suitability index (SI_2), we assigned suitability value based on tree age and ELT. Wood thrush abundance varies by forest age with a peak in early to mid-successional forest, a decline, and then an increase

in mature deciduous or mixed forest (Kahl et al. 1985). In Missouri, the density of breeding birds did not vary in regeneration (0-10 years of age), sapling (11-20 years of age), and pole and sawtimber (>20 years of age) within clearcutting sites, but was higher than uncut sites (Thompson et al. 1992). Also in Missouri, wood thrush density was greater in even-aged treatments compared to control sites 2-3 years after harvest, suggesting wood thrush use mature forest that includes some disturbance (Gram et al. 2003). Wood thrush abundance and density also varied with respect to slope. In southern Illinois, the number of wood thrush detected in ravines was greater than on ridges (Table 1 in Robinson and Robinson 1999), possibly due to differences in moisture conditions and subsequent effects on forage availability and understory development.

We ranked ELTs based on slope and moisture and multiplied that ranking by an age function to determine the suitability value. We ranked ELTs as follows: north and east slopes and bottomlands = 1.00, mesic ridges = 0.75, and dry ridges and south and west slopes = 0.50 based on Robinson and Robinson (1999). All forested stands 11-40 years of age received a suitability value corresponding to the ELT rank described above (Fig. 23). For stands 41-90 years of age, we multiplied the ELT ranking by an age function:

$$SI_2 = 4 - 0.012 \times treeage + 0.001 \times treeage^2$$

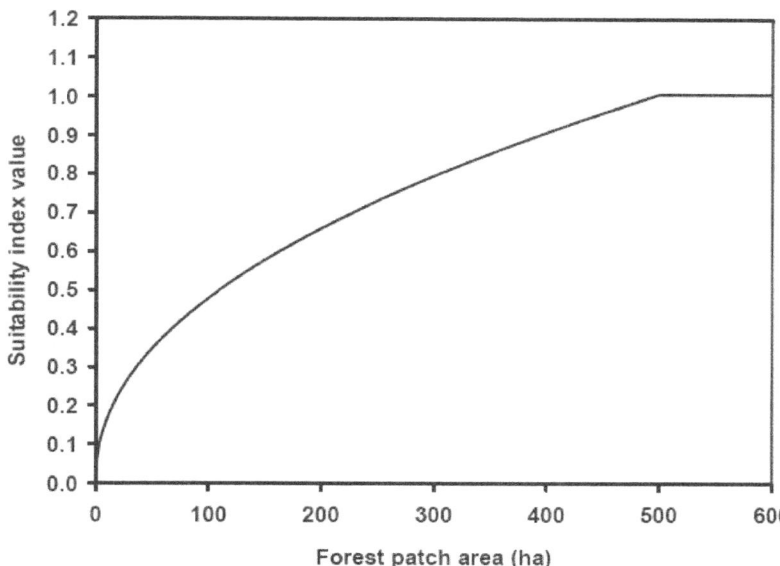

Figure 24.—Wood thrush habitat suitability as a function of deciduous forest area. Suitability value (SI_3) = 0.00 at 1.0 ha and SI_3 = 1.00 for patches >500 ha (from Table 5, Robbins et al. 1989).

to reduce suitability value of mid-successional forests. Forest stands >91 years of age received a suitability value corresponding to the ELT rank (Fig. 23).

In the third suitability index (SI_3), we addressed known forest area requirements. Wood thrushes have been detected in forest fragments as small as 0.2 ha (Robbins et al. 1989) and have successfully nested in 3-ha fragments (Friesen et al. 1999), but nest success is typically higher in larger fragments and contiguous forests. In rural Pennsylvania, nesting success in forest fragments less than 80 ha in size was usually below a sustainable level (Hoover et al. 1995). Robbins et al. (1989) suggested that the minimum area required for breeding was 1.0 ha, with a maximum probability of occurrence at 500 ha. Mueller et al. (1999) estimated forest patch size requirement for 500 breeding pairs was 2800 ha. We developed a suitability function based on the 1-ha minimum area required for occupancy in the Middle Atlantic States (Robbins et al. 1989) (Fig. 24). Although percentage forest in the landscape may be a better metric of habitat suitability than patch size, we lacked data on 1) breeding as a function of percentage forest; and 2) effective landscape size (e.g., size of moving window) in which to evaluate percentage forest. Instead, we fit a power function such that SI_3 = 0.01 for forest patch size = 1 ha, SI_3 = 0.50 for forest patch size = 100 ha, and SI_3 = 1.00 for forest patches ≥500 ha:

$$SI_3 = 0.0568 \times patchsize^{(0.4626)}$$

In the fourth (SI_4) and fifth suitability indexes (SI_5), we addressed the interspersion of post-fledging habitat and breeding habitat. Recent studies indicate juvenile (Anders et al. 1998, Vega Rivera et al. 1998) and adult wood thrush (Thompson et al. 1992, Pagen et al. 2000, Gram et al. 2003) used early successional and mature forest during breeding and post-breeding. Juvenile wood thrush used early successional forest (<30 years of age), including abandoned farms, roadsides, and forest openings, and use shifted to mature deciduous forest late in the post-fledging period (Vega Rivera et al. 1998). Survival of post-fledging juvenile wood thrush increased with an increase in shrub density associated with mid-successional or edge habitats within forest fragments in Missouri (Fink 2003). For juveniles, the distance between natal area and first dispersal sites varied, but averaged 1.5 ± 0.3 km in Virginia (Vega Rivera et al. 1998) and 2.2 ± 0.3 km in Georgia (Lang et al. 2002). In Missouri, the mean distance for first dispersal was 824.5 m, and total average dispersal distance was 1067 m (Fink 2003). We used SI_4 to assign suitability value to cells with stands 11-40 years of age. We applied a moving window (SI_5) with a 1-km radius to SI_4 and determined the proportion of 11-40 year old habitat in the window. We assumed the minimum suitability value was 0.10 irregardless of the proportion of post-fledging habitat within the moving window. We also assumed that the maximum suitability value was reached when the proportion of post-fledging habitat = 0.20. If the proportion of post-fledging habitat

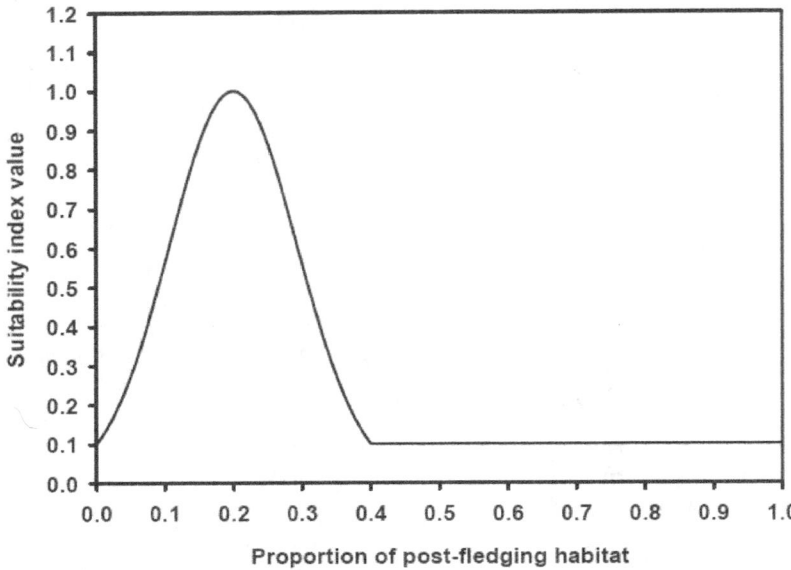

Figure 25.—Wood thrush habitat suitability based on the proportion of post-fledging habitat within 1 km of natal site. Suitability value (SI_5) = 1.00 for landscapes with 20 percent post-fledging habitat. Suitability value (SI_5) = 0.10 for landscapes with >40 percent of post-fledging habitat.

ranged from 0.0-0.40, we assigned suitability value using the function (Fig. 25):

$$SI_5 = e^{-0.5 \times \left(\frac{(ppnPFhab - 0.200)}{0.0932} \right)^2}$$

We developed this equation using a Guassman function such that SI_5 = 0.10 if the proportion of post-fledging habitat = 0.00 or 0.40, and SI_5 = 1.00 if the proportion of post-fledging habitat = 0.20. If the proportion of post-fledging habitat exceeded 0.40, then SI_5 = 0.10. The 1-km moving window was computationally intensive and may be prohibitive when multiple model runs are conducted. In forested landscapes that have diverse and juxtaposed stand ages, SI_5 might be omitted without compromising the general utility of the HSI model. However, knowledge of site-specific conditions and known dispersal distances by wood thrush should be considered before omitting SI_5. We recommend comparison of HSI results with and without SI_5 to aid in the decision process.

The final habitat suitability value was the geometric mean of SI_2, SI_3, and SI_5, multiplied by SI_1 to account for reduced suitability of pines (Fig. 26):

$$HSI = SI_1 \times \left(\sqrt[3]{SI_2 \times SI_3 \times SI_5} \right)$$

Application to test landscape

Suitability index 2, which assigned value based on tree age and ELT, contributed greatly to the heterogeneous pattern observed in the final habitat suitability map. Stand size, homogeneity of tree age within a stand, as well as delineation of stand boundaries will influence the pattern observed when SI_2 is applied to other landscapes. Suitability index 3, which assigned value based on forest patch size, treated continuous canopy gaps (e.g., roads, power lines, and railroads) and nonforested areas as patch boundaries. Natural disturbance from wind and fire, combined with moderate tree harvest, created post-fledging habitat. While the moving-window analysis was computationally intensive due to the large size of the window, it identified several large areas with low interspersion of breeding and post-fledging habitat. When applied to other landscapes, consideration of the known dispersal distances and the level of disturbance should be made before committing computer resources to calculation of SI_5. The final HSI map reflected the diversity of stand ages, sizes, and fire histories.

Worm-eating Warbler

Overview

The worm-eating warbler (*Helmitheros vermivorus*) is a neotropical migratory bird that breeds in eastern North America and winters in Central America and the Greater

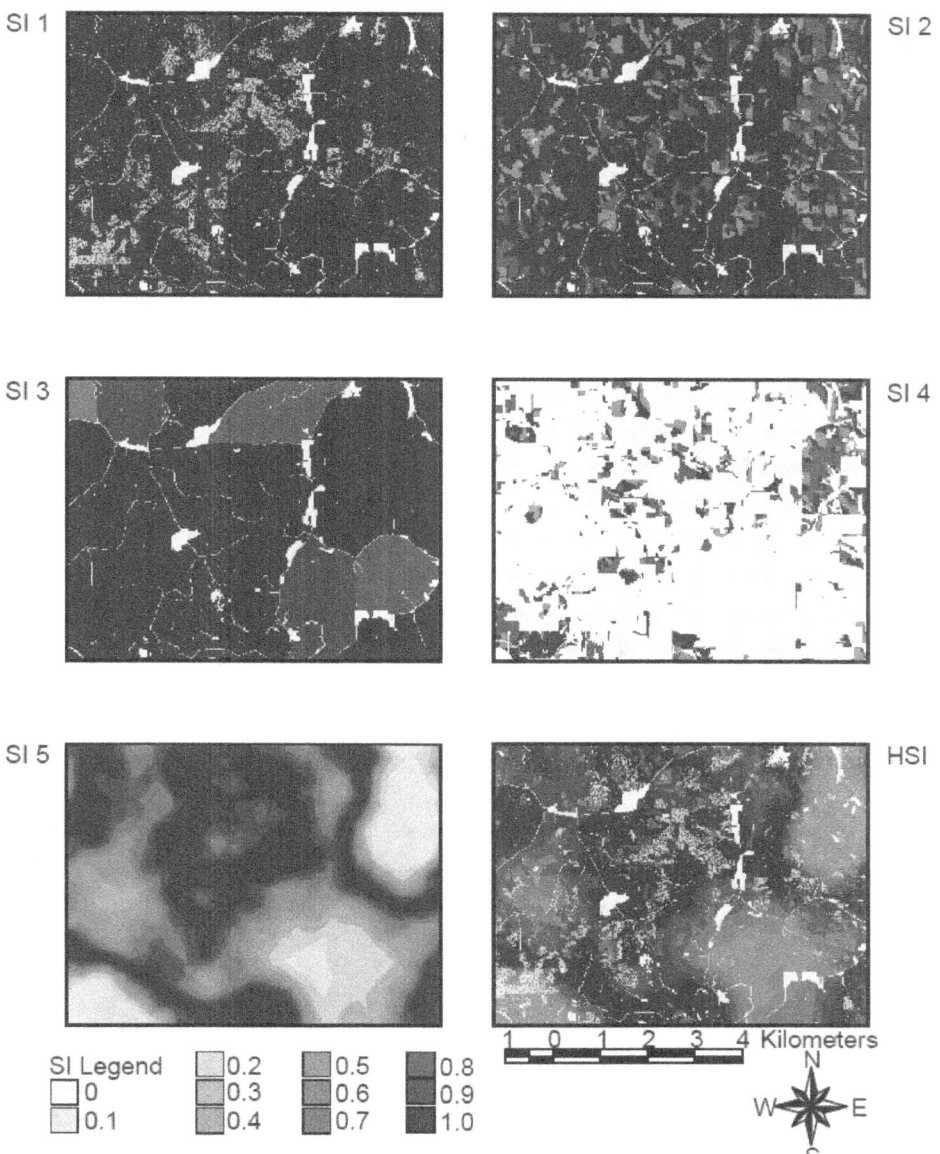

SI 1

SI 2

SI 3

SI 4

SI 5

HSI

SI Legend			
0	0.2	0.5	0.8
0.1	0.3	0.6	0.9
	0.4	0.7	1.0

1 0 1 2 3 4 Kilometers

N
W E
S

Figure 26.—Wood thrush habitat suitability for a 4,281-ha portion of the Hoosier National Forest, Indiana.

Antilles. Worm-eating warblers nest on the ground in large tracts of mature deciduous and mixed-deciduous-coniferous forests with moderate to steep slopes and patches of dense understory shrubs (Hanners and Patton 1998). Existing habitat studies for worm-eating warblers indicate forest area (Robbins et al. 1989, Wenny et al. 1993, Gale et al. 1997), forest edge (Wenny et al. 1993), slope (Robbins et al. 1989, Wenny et al. 1993), prescribed fire (Artman et al. 2001), harvest type and age (Thompson et al. 1992, Robinson and Robinson 1999, Pagen et al. 2000, Gram et al. 2003), as well as canopy height, tree density, moisture gradient, and foliage

density up to 1 m (Robbins et al. 1989), are important habitat features.

HSI model

We developed a worm-eating warbler HSI model for breeding habitat in the Central Hardwoods Region. The first suitability index (SI_1) identified suitable tree species for nesting habitat. Worm-eating warblers rarely occur in pine forest (James and Neal 1986, McNair and Post 1993). Without published information on the use of conifers for nest sites, we identified only deciduous trees as suitable for nesting habitat. We accomplished this

31

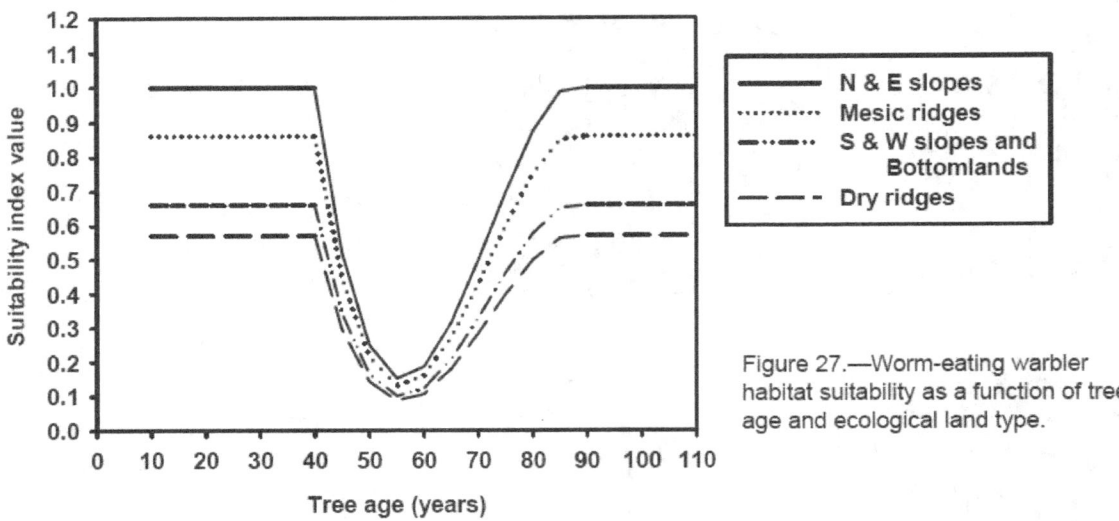

Figure 27.—Worm-eating warbler habitat suitability as a function of tree age and ecological land type.

by evaluating the dominant tree type for each cell and setting SI_1 = 0.00 if the dominant tree type was pine or cedar, and SI_1 = 1.00 otherwise.

In the second suitability index (SI_2), we assigned suitability value based on tree age and ELT. Worm-eating warblers inhabit large tracts of mature forest. In addition to mature forest, worm-eating warblers use early successional forest during the breeding (Robinson and Robinson 1999, Pagen et al. 2000) and post-breeding periods (Pagen et al. 2000). Several studies associate worm-eating warblers with moderate to steep slopes (Mengel 1965, Wenny et al. 1993, Gale et al. 1997, Faaborg et al. 1998), but they also use ridges (Dunn and Garrett 1997, Robinson and Robinson 1999). The distribution of worm-eating warblers also is associated with a moisture gradient, with increased abundance associated with increased moisture (Robbins et al. 1989). Artman et al. (2001) had a higher proportion of territories in mesic than intermediate and xeric sites.

We ranked ELTs based on slope and moisture and multiplied that ranking by an age function to determine the suitability value. We ranked ELTs as follows: ravines (slopes) = 1.00 and ridges = 0.859 (from Table 1 in Robinson and Robinson 1999); mesic sites = 1.00, intermediate sites = 0.660, and xeric sites = 0.226 (from Table 5 in Artman et al. 2001). All forested stands <39 years of age received a suitability value corresponding to

the ELT rank described above (Fig. 27). For stands 40-89 years of age, we multiplied the ELT ranking by an age function:

$$SI_2 = 17.125 - 0.7698 \times treeage + 0.01125 \times treeage^2 - 0.000052083 \times treeage^3$$

to reduce suitability value of mid-successional forests (Fig. 27). Forest stands ≥90 years of age received a suitability value corresponding to the ELT rank described above.

In the third suitability index (SI_3), we addressed known forest area requirements. The worm-eating warbler is considered an area-sensitive species. Robbins et al. (1989) found worm-eating warblers in isolated forest fragments as small as 21 ha in the Middle Atlantic States, but they suggested that the minimum area required for breeding was 150 ha with a maximum probability of occurrence at 3000 ha. Nesting success in small forest fragments (21-56 ha) located within a 70 percent forested landscape (10-km radius) in southern New England was similar to nesting success in a large, unfragmented forest exceeding 750 ha in size (Gale et al. 1997), suggesting that landscape context may ameliorate nesting success in small forest fragments. Worm-eating warblers may also be an edge-sensitive species, but determining whether edge sensitivity occurs in addition to area sensitivity or is an artifact of the distribution of forest remnants (e.g., along moderate to steep slopes unsuitable for agriculture or

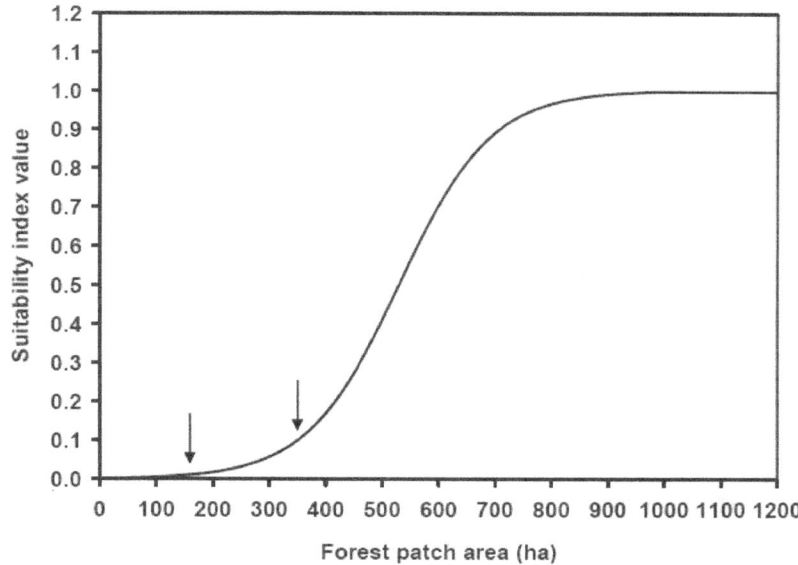

Figure 28.—Worm-eating warbler habitat suitability for breeding as a function of deciduous forest area. Suitability value (SI_3) = 1.00 for patches >1000 ha. Left arrow indicates 150 ha (minimum area requirement, Robbins et al. 1989) and right arrow indicates 340 ha (minimum area requirement, Hayden et al. 1985, Wenny et al. 1993).

development) is an area for further research. In the oak-hickory forests of central Missouri, worm-eating warblers did not occupy a 300-ha isolated forest with over 40 percent forest edge, but occupied an isolated forest of 340 ha with less than 10 percent forest edge (Wenny et al. 1993). Worm-eating warblers bred in an 800-ha forest with less than 10 percent forest edge that was connected to forest along the Missouri River (Wenny et al. 1993).

We developed a suitability function based on the minimum area (150 ha) required for occupancy in the Middle Atlantic States (Robbins et al. 1989) and in Missouri (340 ha) (Wenny et al. 1993) (Fig. 28). For forest patches 0-1000 ha, we assigned suitability using the following function:

$$SI_3 = \frac{1.0032}{\left(1 + e^{((-patchsize-530 1425)/81 8617)}\right)}$$

We developed this equation by fitting a sigmoid function such that SI_3 = 0.01 for 150-ha patches, SI_3 = 0.10 for 340-ha patches, and SI_3 = 1.00 for patches ≥1000 ha.

In the fourth suitability index (SI_4), we reduced suitability value based on fire history for the previous decade. Worm-eating warblers nest on the ground in depressions along steep slopes (Gale 1995) and thus are susceptible to the effects of fire on nest habitat. Site moisture levels may mitigate the initial effects of fire, but

the proportion of breeding territories and the density of adults declines in the first breeding season post-burn (Artman et al. 2001). Over time, additional fires result in a continued decline in density with no recovery to preburn conditions observed 1 year post fire (Artman et al. 2001). Aquilani et al. (2003) reported no difference in worm-eating warbler abundance in unburned and burned areas 1-4 years post-burn, suggesting that the effects of fire may be relatively short-lived. We accounted for the effects of fire that extend several years post-burn but did not completely devalue the habitat for the entire decade because our model input consisted of a fire history for the previous decade. We assigned a suitability value of 0.50 to a cell where fire occurred during the previous decade and 1.00 to unburned cells. In applications with shorter time steps (e.g., annual instead of decade), SI_4 should be adjusted to increase the fire penalty. Additionally, we assumed fires of different intensities affected worm-eating warblers similarly and assigned a single suitability value based on the presence of fire regardless of intensity. However, SI_4 may be adjusted to assign suitability value based on fire intensity.

The final habitat suitability value was the geometric mean of SI_1, SI_2, and SI_3, multiplied by SI_4, to account for reduced suitability due to fire (Fig. 29):

$$HSI = \left(\sqrt[3]{SI_1 \times SI_2 \times SI_3}\right) \times SI_4$$

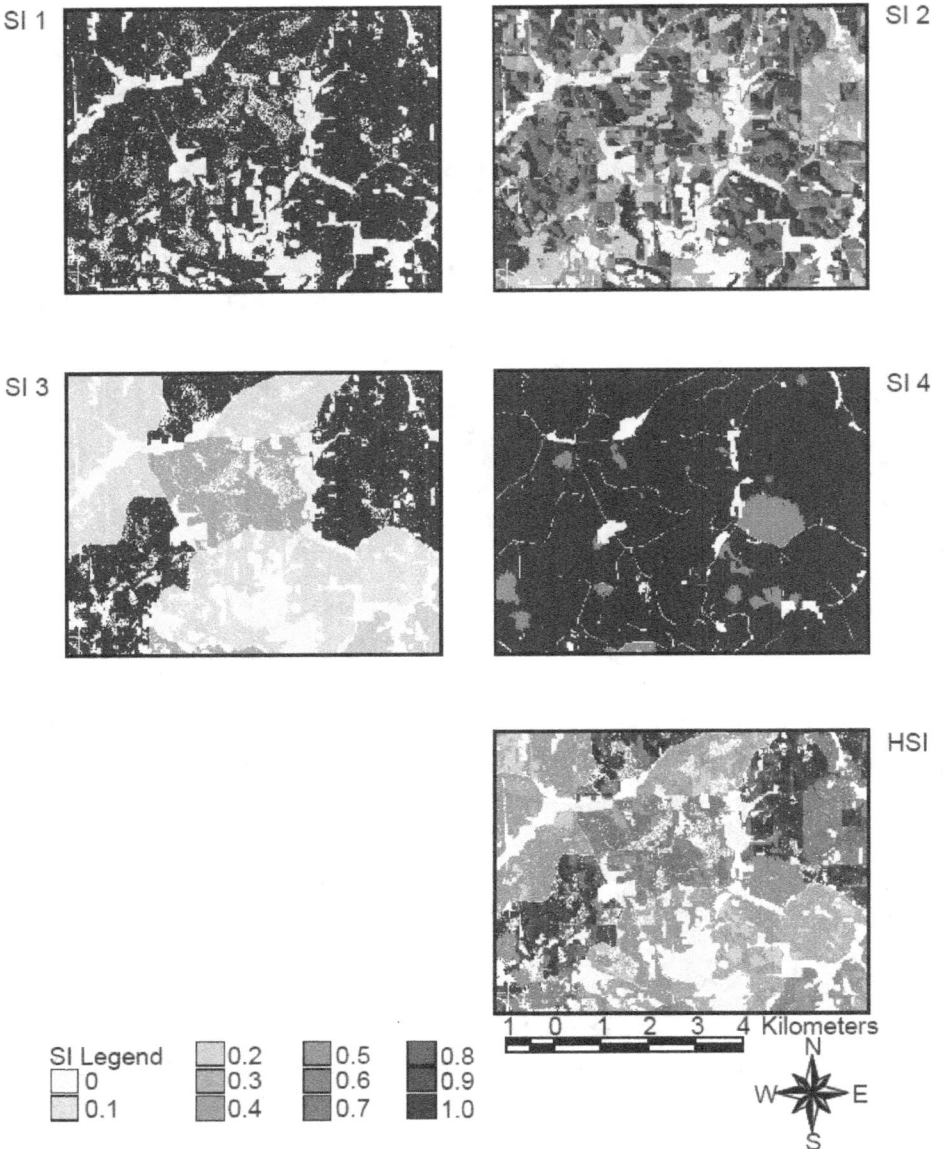

SI 1

SI 2

SI 3

SI 4

HSI

1 0 1 2 3 4 Kilometers

SI Legend
0
0.1
0.2
0.3
0.4
0.5
0.6
0.7
0.8
0.9
1.0

N
W E
S

Figure 29.—Worm-eating warbler habitat suitability for breeding on a 4,281-ha portion of the Hoosier National Forest, Indiana.

Application to test landsape

Suitability index 2, which assigned value based on tree age and ELT, contributed greatly to the heterogeneous pattern observed in the final habitat suitability map. Stand size, homogeneity of tree age within a stand, as well as delineation of stand boundaries will influence the pattern observed when SI_2 is applied to other landscapes. Suitability index 3, which assigned value based on forest patch size, treated continuous canopy gaps (e.g., roads, power lines, and railroads) and nonforested areas as patch boundaries. Prescribed burning (SI_4) reduced suitability for approximately 5 percent of the landscape. The final

HSI map reflects the diversity of stand ages, sizes, and fire histories.

Yellow-breasted Chat

Overview

The yellow-breasted chat (*Icteria virens*) is a migratory bird that breeds in North America and winters in Central America. Chats are considered a disturbance-dependent shrubland species (Eckerle and Thompson 2001). In the eastern and Midwestern United States, chats are found in early second-growth forest and shrubs in abandoned agricultural fields, clear-cuts, power-line

Table 4.—Nesting habitat suitability by tree age and ecological land type (ELT) for yellow-breasted chats. We assigned maximum suitability (SI$_1$ = 1.00) to stands 1-10 years of age on all ELTs. Suitability declined to zero for stands 11-40 years of age on the two driest ELTs. Stands >11 years on mesic ELTs and stands >41 years on all ELTs had no suitability (SI$_1$ = 0.00).

| | SI$_1$ | | | | |
Stand Age	Dry Ridges	S and W Slopes	Mesic Ridges	N and E Slopes	Bottomlands
1 – 10	1.00	1.00	1.00	1.00	1.00
11 – 20	0.50	0.50	0.00	0.00	0.00
21 – 30	0.30	0.30	0.00	0.00	0.00
31 – 40	0.10	0.10	0.00	0.00	0.00
≥41	0.00	0.00	0.00	0.00	0.00

corridors, fencerows, forest edges and openings (Eckerle and Thompson 2001). Like other shrubland bird species, the yellow-breasted chat is both area and edge sensitive (Annand and Thompson 1997, Woodward et al. 2001, Rodewald and Vitz 2005). Because no previous HSI model existed for yellow-breasted chats, we developed a new model based on reported ecological relationships gathered from extensive literature review.

HSI model

We developed a yellow-breasted chat HSI model for breeding habitat in the Central Hardwoods Region. The first suitability index (SI$_1$) identified early successional forest habitat and old fields for nesting habitat. Yellow-breasted chats nest in low, dense, deciduous and coniferous vegetation (Eckerle and Thompson 2001), and use old fields when woody plants invade and reach peak densities in dense shrub thickets (Shugart and James 1973). Chats also colonize clearcuts and power-line corridors (Kroodsma 1982). Use of old fields in Indiana declined when saplings shaded 50 percent of the ground (Kahl et al. 1985). In Virginia, chats were present in mixed-oak stands 3-12 years of age (Connor and Adkisson 1975). In southeast Missouri, chat numbers were higher in clearcut areas than shelterwood, group selection, or single-tree selection forest regeneration methods (Annand and Thompson 1997).

We assigned a suitability value to each cell based on tree age and ELT (Table 4). All forested stands <10 years of age received SI$_1$ = 1.00 for both mesic and dry ELTs. On the two driest ELTs, suitability value declined as tree age increased to 40 years. Trees ≥41 years of age on dry ELTs and trees ≥11 years on mesic ELTs had SI$_1$ = 0.00.

In the second suitability index (SI$_2$), we addressed an early successional forest area requirement. The minimum patch size used by yellow-breasted chats varies by region and type of opening, but chats are rarely detected in patches <0.40 ha (Robinson and Robinson 1999). The minimum patch size for breeding may be larger than 0.40 ha observed by (Robinson and Robinson 1999). For example, chats nested in uneven-aged openings of 0.14-0.58 ha in Missouri, but nested in higher densities in even-aged openings of 3-13 ha (Gram et al. 2003). Patch size in old fields surrounded by oak-hickory forest ranged from 2.4-16.3 ha in Missouri (Burhans and Thompson 1999). We developed a breeding suitability function for patches of contiguous cells where SI$_1$ >0.00 and applied the function to patches 0.01–5 ha in size (Fig. 30):

$$SI_2 = \frac{1.0442}{\left(1 + e^{((-patchsize - 3.3389)/0.5965)}\right)}$$

We developed this equation by fitting a sigmoid function such that SI$_2$ = 0.01 for 0.4 ha patches, SI$_2$ = 0.10 for 2.0 ha patches, and SI$_3$ = 1.00 for patches ≥5 ha. Patches 0.01 ha had SI$_2$ = 0.00.

In the third suitability index (SI$_3$), we reduced the value of early successional habitat adjacent to mid- to late-succesional forest and urban edges. Yellow-breasted chats are considered edge sensitive, with reduced captures of both hatch-year and after-hatch-year chats near mature-forest edges (Rodewald and Vitz 2005). Edge avoidance likely occurs for a variety of reasons, including reduction in nest predation rates; yellow-breasted chat nests located within 20 m of a forested edge had higher daily predation rates than nests located ≥20 m from a forested edge

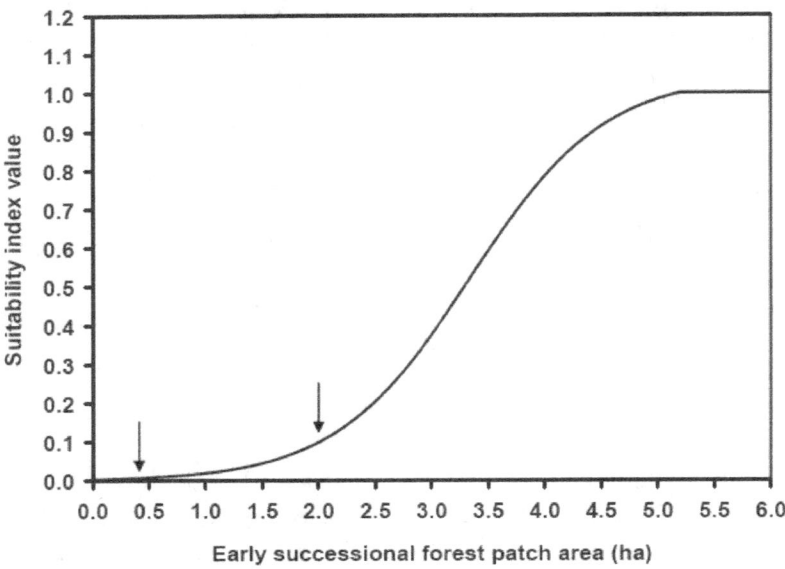

Figure 30.—Yellow-breasted chat habitat suitability for breeding as a function of early successional forest area. Suitability value (SI_2) = 0.00 for patches ≤0.01 ha and SI_3 = 1.00 for patches ≥5 ha. Left arrow indicates 0.4 ha (minimum area requirement, Robinson and Robinson 1999) and right arrow indicates 2.0 ha (minimum area requirement; SVE Panel 2002).

(Woodward et al. 2001). We applied a moving window with a 20-m radius to cells with SI_1 >0.00. The moving window reduced the value of cells located <20 m from a nonsuitable edge (SI_3 = 0.00), but retained the value assigned in SI_1 for cells located >20 m from a nonsuitable edge (SI_3 = SI_1).

The final habitat suitability value was the geometric mean of SI_1 and SI_2, multiplied by SI_3, to impose the edge-sensitivity penalty (Fig. 31):

$$HSI = \left(\sqrt[2]{SI_1 \times SI_2} \right) \times SI_3$$

Application to test landscape

The first suitability index identified numerous patches of early successional forest ranging in size from 0.10-7.52 ha (Fig. 31). Imposing the minimum patch size constraint removed only patches created by small-scale disturbance (e.g., treefall gaps) and identified 10 patches greater than 5 ha (SI_2 = 1.00). The edge penalty had a large effect on the amount of suitable habitat. Small patches and irregularly shaped patches (e.g., linear) had a higher proportion of habitat lost to the edge penalty than large, regularly shaped patches (e.g., round). In addition to patch size and shape, harvest type also will influence the amount of habitat lost to the edge penalty. Harvest techniques that retain trees in older size classes (e.g., from selective harvest, shelterwood) will lose a greater amount of habitat to the edge penalty than even-aged techniques.

CONCLUSIONS

The landscape-level, GIS-based habitat suitability models we developed represent the state of our knowledge, given tradeoffs between model complexity and model utility. We quantified the suitability relationships using information gained from empirical studies and expert opinion. Some models had detailed functions describing suitability relationships because existing data supported the complexity of those relationships, whereas other models had sigmoid or linear functions that described the same relationship. For example, both the wood thrush and the worm-eating models had age × ELT-specific functions (Fig. 23, Fig. 27) supported by point count, nesting, mist-netting, and radio-telemetry data, for both nesting and post-fledging habitat use. Contrast this with the American woodcock age × ELT functions (Fig. 3), which were developed from a more limited database. The resulting suitability relationship clearly lacks the specificity of the wood thrush or worm-eating warbler functions. The importance of data collection during different parts of the breeding season cannot be overemphasized. Additional research may reveal whether the functions used in other models are equally complex or as simple as we portrayed them. In this way, the HSI models reveal the limitations of existing data and suggest areas where additional research efforts may be focused.

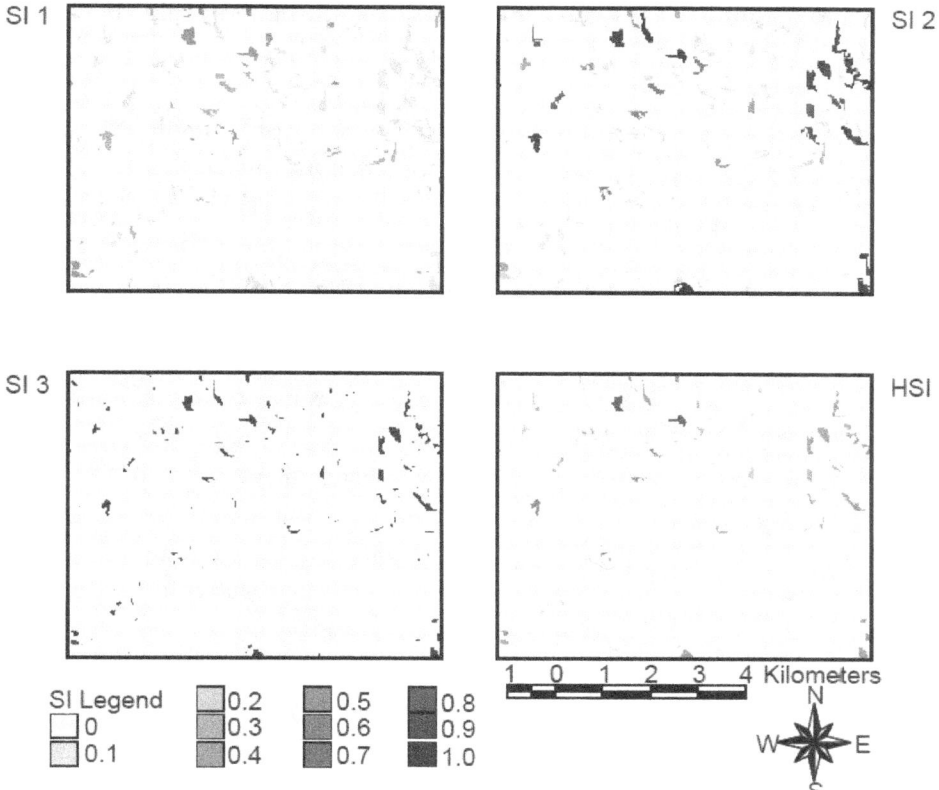

SI 1

SI 2

SI 3

HSI

1 0 1 2 3 4 Kilometers

SI Legend
0
0.1
0.2
0.3
0.4
0.5
0.6
0.7
0.8
0.9
1.0

Figure 31.—Yellow-breasted chat habitat suitability for breeding on a 4,281-ha portion of the Hoosier National Forest, Indiana.

ACKNOWLEDGMENTS

The development of these models benefited greatly from the knowledge and comments freely shared by many people. Our gratitude extends to the following: all participants of the Species Viability Evaluation Panel; Cynthia Basile, Clark McCreedy, Judi Perez, Kelle Reynolds and Tom Thake of the Hoosier National Forest; Sybill Amelon, John Faaborg and the University of Missouri Avian Ecology Lab, Mike Larson, Neil Sullivan and Mark Yates. We thank Dirk Burhans, John Dunning, D. Todd Farrand, Mark Ryan and John Tirpak for comments that improved this manuscript. The U.S. Forest Service Northern Research Station and the University of Missouri provided financial and logistic support for this project.

LITERATURE CITED

Adams, J.P. 2005. **Home range and behavior of the timber rattlesnake *(Crotalus horridus).*** Huntington, WV: Marshall University. 104 p. M.S. thesis.

Aldridge, R.D.; Brown, W.S. 1995. **Male reproductive cycle, age at maturity, and cost of reproduction in the timber rattlesnake *(Crotalus horridus).*** Journal of Herpetology. 29: 399-407.

Anders, A.D.; Faaborg, J.; Thompson, F.R., III. 1998. **Postfledging dispersal, habitat use, and home-range size of juvenile wood thrushes.** The Auk. 115: 349-358.

Andrews, K.M.; Gibbons, J.W. 2005. **How do highways influence snake movement? Behavioral responses to roads and vehicles.** Copeia. 2005: 772-782.

Annand, E.M.; Thompson, F.R., III. 1997. **Forest bird response to regeneration practices in central hardwood forests.** Journal of Wildlife Management. 61: 159-171.

Aquilani, S.M.; Morrell, T.E.; LeBlanc, D.C. 2003. **Breeding bird communities in burned and unburned sites in a mature Indiana oak forest.** Proceedings of the Indiana Academy of Science. 112: 186-191.

Archibald, H.L. 1975. **Temporal patterns of spring space use by ruffed grouse.** Journal of Wildlife Management. 39: 472-481.

Artman, V.L.; Sutherland, E.K.; Downhower, J.F. 2001. **Prescribed burning to restore mixed-oak communities in southern Ohio: effects on breeding-bird populations.** Conservation Biology. 15: 1423-1434.

Backs, S.E.; Sintz, G.; Danner, C.; Savery, E.J. 1981. **A quantitative method for evaluating bobwhite quail habitat in Indiana. Final report.** Indianapolis, IN: Indiana Department of Natural Resources. 20 p. [Unpublished wildlife report, Federal Aid in Wildlife Restoration Project W-26-R-12.]

Backs, S.E. 1984. **Ruffed grouse restoration in Indiana.** In: Robinson, W.L., ed.; Ruffed grouse management: state of the art in the early 1980's. Symposium proceedings, 45th Midwest Fish and Wildlife Conference; 1983 December 5-7; St. Louis, MO. Bloomington, IN: Wildlife Society and Ruffed Grouse Society, North Central Section: 37-58.

Bailey, R.G. 1996. **Ecosystem geography.** New York: Springer. 204 p.

Bajema, R.A.; Lima, S.L. 2001. **Landscape-level analyses of Henslow's sparrow (_Ammodramus henslowii_) abundance in reclaimed coal mine grasslands.** American Midland Naturalist. 145: 288-298.

Banner, A.; Schaller, S. 2001. **USFWS Gulf of Maine watershed habitat analysis.** Falmouth, ME: U.S. Fish and Wildlife Service. Available from: http://www.fws.gov/r5gomp/gom/habitatstudy/Gulf_of_Maine_Watershed_Habitat_Analysis.htm

Bartholomew, R.M. 1967. **A study of the winter activity of bobwhites through the use of radio telemetry.** Occas. Pap. No. 17. Kalamazoo, MI: C. C. Adams Center for Ecological Studies. 25 p.

Basile, C.; Islam, K. 2001. **Territory size and characteristics of Cerulean warblers in southern Indiana.** In: Indiana Academy of Sciences 117th annual meeting; 2001 November 9; Fort Wayne, IN: Indianapolis, IN: Indiana Academy of Sciences. Abstract.

Brack, V.W., Jr. 1983. **The nonhibernating ecology of bats in Indiana with emphasis on the endangered Indiana bat, _Myotis sodalis_.** West Lafayette, IN: Purdue University. 280 p. Ph.D. dissertation.

Brady, S.J.; Flather, C.H.; Church, K.E.; Schenck, E.W. 1993. **Correlates of northern bobwhite distribution and abundance with land-use characteristics in Kansas.** Proceedings of the National Quail Symposium. 3: 115-125.

Brennan, L.A. 1999. **Northern bobwhite (_Colinus virginianus_).** In: Poole, A.; Gill, F., eds. The Birds of North America. Vol. 10, No. 397. Philadelphia, PA: The Birds of North America, Inc. 28 p.

Brown, W.S. 1991. **Female reproductive ecology in a northern population of the timber rattlesnake, _Crotalus horridus_.** Herpetologica. 47: 101-115.

Brown, W.S. 1992. **Emergence, ingress, and seasonal captures at dens of northern timber rattlesnakes, _Crotalus horridus_.** In: Campbell, J.A.; Brodie, E.D., eds. Biology of the pitvipers. Tyler, TX: Selva Press: 251-258.

Brown, W.S. 1993. **Biology, status, and management of the timber rattlesnake (*Crotalus horridus*): a guide for conservation.** Herpetological Circular No. 22. [Place of publication unknown]: Society for the Study of Amphibians and Reptiles. 84 p.

Brown, W.S.; Pyle, D.W.; Greene, K.R.; Friedlaender, J.B. 1982. **Movements and temperature relationships of timber rattlesnakes (*Crotalus horridus*) in northeastern New York.** Journal of Herpetology. 16: 151-161.

Bump, G.R.; Darrow, W.; Edminster, F.C.; Crissey, W.F. 1947. **The ruffed grouse: life history, propagation, and management.** Albany, NY: New York State Conservation Department. 915 p.

Burger, L.W., Jr.; Linder, E.T.; Hamrick, R. 2004. **A regional northern bobwhite habitat model for planning and prioritization of habitat restoration in the Central Hardwoods Bird Conservation Region.** Final report to the American Bird Conservancy. Mississippi State, MS: Mississippi State University. 39 p.

Burhans, D.E. 2002. **Conservation assessment: Henslow's Sparrow *Ammodramus henslowii*.** Gen. Tech. Rep. NC-226. St. Paul, MN: U.S. Department of Agriculture, Forest Service, North Central Research Station. 46 p.

Burhans, D.E.; Thompson, F.R., III. 1999. **Habitat patch size and nesting success of yellow-breasted chats.** Wilson Bulletin. 111: 210-215.

Cade, B.S.; Sousa, P.J. 1985. **Habitat suitability models: ruffed grouse.** Biological Report. 82(10.86). Washington, DC: U.S. Fish and Wildlife Service. 31 p.

Callahan, E.V.; Drobney, R.D.; Clawson, R.L. 1997. **Selection of summer roosting sites by Indiana bats (*Myotis sodalis*) in Missouri.** Journal of Mammalogy. 78: 818-825.

Carter, T.C.; Carroll, S.K.; Feldhammer, G.A. 2000. **Preliminary work on maternity colonies of Indiana bat (*Myotis sodalis*) in Illinois.** Bat Research News. 41: 112-113.

Clark, B.K.; Bowles, J.B.; Clark, B.S. 1987a. **Summer occurrence of the Indiana bat, Keen's bat, evening bat, silver-haired bat, and eastern pipistrelle in Iowa.** Proceedings of the Iowa Academy of Science. 94: 89-93.

Clark, B.K.; Bowles, J.B.; Clark, B.S. 1987b. **Summer status of the endangered Indiana bat in Iowa.** American Midland Naturalist. 118: 32-39.

Connor, R.N.; Adkisson, C.S. 1975. **Effects of clearcutting on the diversity of breeding birds.** Journal of Forestry. 73: 781-785.

Cope, J.B., Richter, A.R.; Mills, R.S. 1974. **Concentrations of the endangered Indiana bat, *Myotis sodalis*, in Wayne County, Indiana.** Proceedings of the Indiana Academy of Science. 83: 482-484.

Cully, J.F., Jr.; Michaels, H.L. 2000. **Henslow's sparrow habitat associations on Kansas tallgrass prairie.** Wilson Bulletin. 112: 115-123.

Dailey, T.V. 1989. **Bobwhite quail investigations: modeling bobwhite quail habitat relationships on four central Missouri wildlife management areas.** Columbia, MO: Missouri Department of Conservation. 19 p. [Unpublished wildlife report, Federal Aid in Wildlife Restoration Project W-13-R-43.]

DeStefano, S.; Rusch, D.H. 1984. **Characteristics of ruffed grouse drumming sites in northeastern Wisconsin.** Transactions of the Wisconsin Academy of Sciences, Arts and Letters. 72: 177-182.

DeVos, T.; Mueller, B.S. 1993. **Reproductive ecology of northern bobwhite in Florida.** In: Church, K.E.; Dailey, T.V., eds. Proceedings of the third national quail symposium; 1992 July 14-17; Kansas City, MO. Pratt, KS: Kansas Department of Wildlife and Parks: 83-89.

Dijak, W.D.; Rittenhouse, C.D.; Larson, M.A.; Thompson, F.R., III; Millspaugh, J.J. 2007. **Landscape habitat suitability index software.** Journal of Wildlife Management. 71(2) In press.

Dimmick, R.W. 1972. **The influence of controlled burning on nesting patterns of bobwhite in west Tennessee.** Proceedings of the annual conference of the Southeast Fish and Wildlife Agencies. 25: 149-155.

Donovan, T.M.; Jones, P.W.; Annand, E.M.; Thompson, F.R., III. 1997. **Variation in local-scale edge effects: mechanisms and landscape context.** Ecology. 78: 2064-2075.

Dunford, R.D.; Owen, R.B., Jr. 1973. **Summer behavior of immature radio-equipped woodcock in central Maine.** Journal of Wildlife Management. 37: 462-469.

Dunn, J.L.; Garrett, K.L. 1997. **A field guide to warblers of North America.** New York: Houghton Mifflin. 672 p.

Dwyer, T.J.; McAuley, D.G.; Derleth, E.L. 1983. **Woodcock singing-ground counts and habitat changes in the northeastern United States.** Journal of Wildlife Management. 47: 772-779.

Eckerle, K.P.; Thompson, C.F. 2001. **Yellow-breasted chat (*Icteria virens*).** In: Poole, A.; Gill, F., eds. The Birds of North America. Vol. 15, No. 575. Philadelphia, PA: The Birds of North America, Inc. 28 p.

Faaborg, J.; F.R. Thompson, III; Robinson, S.K.; Donovan, T.M.; Whitehead, D.R.; Brawn, J.D. 1998. **Understanding fragmented Midwestern landscapes: the future.** In: Marzluff, J.M.; Sallabanks, R., eds. Avian conservation: research and management. Washington, DC: Island Press: 193-207.

Fan, Z.F.; Larsen, D.R.; Shifley, S.R.; Thompson, F.R., III. 2003. **Estimating cavity tree abundance by stand age and basal area, Missouri, USA.** Forest Ecology and Management. 179: 231-242.

Farmer, A.H.; Cade, B.S.; Stauffer, D.F. 2002. **Evaluation of a habitat suitability index model.** In: Kurta, A.; Kennedy, J., eds. The Indiana bat: biology and management of an endangered species. Austin, TX: Bat Conservation International: 172-179.

Fink, M.L. 2003. **Post-fledging ecology of juvenile wood thrush in fragmented and contiguous landscapes.** Columbia, MO: University of Missouri. 146 p. Ph.D. dissertation.

Fitch, H.S. 1999. **A Kansas snake community: composition and changes over 50 years.** Melbourne, FL: Krieger Publishing Company. 165 p.

Friesen, L.E.; Wyatt, V.E.; Cadman, M.D. 1999. **Pairing success of wood thrushes in a fragmented agricultural landscape.** Wilson Bulletin. 111: 279-281.

Gale, G.A. 1995. **Habitat selection in the worm-eating warbler (*Helmitheros vermivorus*): testing on different spatial scales.** Storrs, CT: University of Connecticut. Ph.D. dissertation.

Gale, G.A.; Hanners, L.A.; Patton, S.R. 1997. **Reproductive success of worm-eating warblers in a forested landscape.** Conservation Biology. 11: 246-250.

Garber, J.W.; Graber, R.R.; Kirk, E.L. 1983. **Illinois birds: wood warblers.** Biological Notes No. 118. Champaign, IL: Illinois Natural History Survey.

Gardner, J.E.; Garner, J.D.; Hofmann, J.E. 1991. **Summer roost selection and roosting behavior of *Myotis sodalis* (Indiana bat) in Illinois.** Final Report. Champaign, IL: Illinois Natural History Survey and Illinois Department of Conservation. 56 p.

Gardner, J.E.; Hofmann, J.E.; Garner, J.D. 1996. **Summer distribution of the federally endangered Indiana Bat (*Myotis sodalis*) in Illinois.** Transactions of the Illinois Academy of Science. 89: 187-196.

Gibson, S.; Kingsbury, B. 2002. **Ecology and conservation of the timber rattlesnake (*Crotalus horridus*) in Indiana.** Report for Indiana Department of Natural Resources. Fort Wayne, IN: Indiana-Purdue University, Center for Reptile and Amphibian Conservation and Management. 46 p.

Gram, W.K.; Porneluzi, P.A.; Clawson, R.L.; Faaborg, J.; Richter, S.C. 2003. **Effects of experimental forest management on density and nesting success of bird species in Missouri Ozark forests.** Conservation Biology. 17: 1324-1337.

Gudlin, M.J.; Dimmick, R.W. 1984. **Habitat utilization by ruffed grouse transplanted from Wisconsin to west Tennessee.** In: Robinson, W.L., ed.; Ruffed grouse management: state of the art in the early 1980's. Symposium proceedings, 45th Midwest Fish and Wildlife Conference; 1983 December 5-7; St. Louis, MO. Bloomington, IN: Wildlife Society and Ruffed Grouse Society, North Central Section: 75-88.

Gullion, G.W.; King, R.T.; Marshall, W.H. 1962. **Male ruffed grouse and thirty years of forest management on the Cloquet Forest Research Center, Minnesota.** Journal of Forestry. 60: 617-622.

Gustafson, E.J.; Murphy, D.W.; Crow, T.R. 2001. **Using a GIS model to assess terrestrial salamander response to alternative forest management plans.** Journal of Environmental Management. 63: 281-292.

Guthery, F.S. 1997. **A philosophy of habitat management for northern bobwhites.** Journal of Wildlife Management. 61: 291-301.

Gutzwiller, K.J.; Kinsley, K.R.; Storm, G.L.; Tzilkowski, W.M.; Wakeley, J.S. 1983. **Relative value of vegetation structure and species composition for identifying American woodcock breeding habitat.** Journal of Wildlife Management. 47: 535-540.

Hall, J.S. 1962. **A life history and taxonomic study of the Indiana bat, *Myotis sodalis*.** Scientific Publication No. 12. Reading, PA: Reading Public Museum and Art Gallery. 68 p.

Hamel, P.B. 1992. **Cerulean warbler, *Dendroica cerulea*.** In: Schneider, K.J.; Pence, D.M., eds. Migratory nongame birds of management concern in the Northeast. Newtown Corner, MA: U.S. Fish and Wildlife Service: 385-400.

Hamel, P.B. 2000a. **Cerulean warbler (*Dendroica cerulea*).** In: Poole, A.; Gill, F. eds. The Birds of North America. Vol. 13, No. 511. Philadelphia, PA: The Birds of North America, Inc. 20 p.

Hamel, P.B. 2000b. **Cerulean warbler status assessment.** Minneapolis, MN: U.S. Fish and Wildlife Service. 141 p.

Hands, H.M.; Drobney, R.D.; Ryan, M.R. 1989. **Status of the Henslow's sparrow in the northcentral United States.** Columbia, MO: Missouri Cooperative Fish and Wildlife Research Unit. 12 p.

Hanners, L.A.; Patton, S.R. 1998. **Worm-eating warbler (*Helmitheros vermivorus*).** In: Poole, A.; Gill, F., eds. The Birds of North America. Volume 10, No. 367. Philadelphia, PA: The Birds of North America, Inc. 20 p.

Harroff, N.K. 1999. **Investigating the status of the Henslow's sparrow in southern Illinois.** Meadowlark. 8: 48-49.

Hayden, T.J.; Faaborg, J.; Clawson, R.L. 1985. **Estimates of minimum area requirements for Missouri forest birds.** Transactions of the Missouri Academy of Science. 19: 11-27.

Herkert, J.R. 1994. **The effects of habitat fragmentation on midwestern grassland bird communities.** Ecological Applications. 4: 461-471.

Herkert, J.R. 2001. **Effects of management practices on grassland birds: Henslow's sparrow.** Jamestown, ND: U S. Geological Survey, Northern Prairie Wildlife Research Center. 17 p.

Herkert, J.R.; Vickery, P.D.; Kroodsma, D.E. 2002. **Henslow's sparrow (*Ammodramus henslowii*).** In:

Poole, A.; Gill, F., eds. The Birds of North America. Vol. 17, No. 672. Philadelphia, PA: The Birds of North America, Inc. 23 p.

Hoover, J.P.; Brittingham, M.C.; Goodrich, L.J. 1995. **Effects of forest patch size on nesting success of wood thrushes.** The Auk. 112: 146-155.

Hudgins, J.E.; Storm, G.L.; Wakeley, J.S. 1985. **Local movements and diurnal-habitat selection by male American woodcock in Pennsylvania.** Journal of Wildlife Management. 49: 614-619.

Humphrey, S.R.; Richter, A.R.; Cope, J.B. 1977. **Summer habitat and ecology of the endangered Indiana bat, *Myotis sodalis*.** Journal of Mammalogy. 58: 334-346.

Hunyadi, B.W. 1984. **Ruffed grouse restoration in Missouri.** In: Robinson, W.L., ed.; Ruffed grouse management: state of the art in the early 1980's. Symposium proceedings, 45th Midwest Fish and Wildlife Conference; 1983 December 5-7; St. Louis, MO. Bloomington, IN: Wildlife Society and Ruffed Grouse Society, North Central Section: 151-168.

James, D.A.; Neal, J.C. 1986. **Arkansas birds: their distribution and abundance.** Fayetteville, AR: University of Arkansas Press. 416 p.

Johnsgard, P.A. 1973. **Grouse and quail of North America.** Lincoln, NE: University of Nebraska Press. 553 p.

Jones, J.K.; Armstrong, D.M.; Choate, J.R. 1985. *Myotis sodalis*, **social myotis.** In: Guide to the mammals of the Plains States. Lincoln, NE: University of Nebraska Press. 371 p.

Kahl, R.B.; Baskett, T.S.; Ellis, J.A.; Burroughs, J.N. 1985. **Characteristics of summer habitats of selected nongame birds in Missouri.** Res. Bull. 1056. Columbia, MO: University of Missouri-Columbia, Agric. Exp. Sta.: 68-71.

Keppie, D.M.; Whiting, R.M., Jr. 1994. **American woodcock (*Scolopax minor*).** In: Poole, A.; Gill, F., eds. The Birds of North America. Vol. 13, No. 100. Philadelphia, PA: The Birds of North America, Inc. 28 p.

Klauber, L.M. 1997. **Rattlesnakes: their habits, life histories, and influence on mankind.** Second edition. Berkeley, CA: University of California Press. 1533 p.

Klaus, N.A.; Buehler, D.A.; Saxton, A.M.. 2005. **Forest management alternatives and songbird breeding habitat on the Cherokee National Forest, Tennessee.** Journal of Wildlife Management. 69: 222-234.

Klute, D.S.; Lovallo, M.J.; Tzilkowski, W.M.; Storm, G.L. 2000. **Determining multiscale habitat and landscape associations for American woodcock in Pennsylvania.** In: McAuley, D.G., et al., eds. Proceedings of the ninth American woodcock symposium. Biological Rep. 16. Laurel, MD: U.S. Fish and Wildlife Service, Patuxent Wildlife Research Center: 42-49.

Krohn, W.B. 1971. **Some patterns of woodcock activities on Maine summer fields.** Wilson Bulletin. 83: 396-407.

Kroodsma, R.L. 1982. **Bird community ecology on power-line corridors in east Tennessee.** Biological Conservation. 23: 79-94.

Kubisiak, J.F. 1984. **The impact of hunting on ruffed grouse populations in the Sandhill Wildlife Area.** In: Robinson, W.L., ed.; Ruffed grouse management: state of the art in the early 1980's. Symposium proceedings, 45th Midwest Fish and Wildlife Conference; 1983 December 5-7; St. Louis, MO. Bloomington, IN: Wildlife Society and Ruffed Grouse Society, North Central Section: 151-168 .

Kubisiak, J.F.; Moulton, J.C.; McCaffery, K.R. 1980. **Ruffed grouse density and habitat relationships in Wisconsin.** Tech. Bull. No. 108. Madison, WI: Wisconsin Department of Natural Resources. 15 p.

Kurta, A. 1995. **Mammals of the Great Lakes region.** Ann Arbor, MI: University of Michigan Press. 392 p.

Kurta, A.; Kath, J.; Smith, E.L.; Foster, R.; Orick, M.W.; Ross, R. 1993a. **A maternity roost of the endangered Indiana bat (*Myotis sodalis*) in an unshaded, hollow, sycamore tree (*Platanus occidentalis*).** American Midland Naturalist. 130: 405-407.

Kurta, A.; King, D.; Teramino, J.A.; Stribley, J.M.; Williams, K.J. 1993b. **Summer roosts of the endangered Indiana bat (*Myotis sodalis*) on the northern edge of its range.** American Midland Naturalist. 129: 132-138.

Kurta, A.; Murray, S.W.; Miller, D.H. 2002. **Roost selection and movements across the summer landscape.** In: Kurta, A.; Kennedy, J., eds. The Indiana bat: biology and management of an endangered species. Austin, TX: Bat Conservation International: 118-129.

Kurta, A.; Williams, K.J.; Mies, R. 1996. **Ecological, behavioral, and thermal observations of a peripheral population of Indiana bats (*Myotis sodalis*).** In: Barclay, R.M.R.; Brigham, R.M., eds. Bats and forests symposium. Victoria, BC: British Columbia Ministry of Forests: 102-117.

Landers, J.L.; Johnson, A.S. 1976. **Bobwhite quail food habits in the southeastern United States with a seed key to important foods.** Misc. Publ. 4. Tallahassee, FL: Tall Timbers Research Station. 90 p.

Landers, J.L.; Mueller, B.S. 1986. **Bobwhite quail management: a habitat approach.** Tallahassee, FL: Tall Timbers Research Station. 39 p.

Lang, J.D.; Powell, L.A.; Krementz, D.G.; Conroy, M.J. 2002. **Wood thrush movements and habitat use: effects of forest management for red-cockaded woodpeckers.** The Auk. 119: 109-124.

Larimer, E.J. 1960. **Winter foods of the bobwhite in southern Illinois.** Biological Notes 42. Champaign, IL: Illinois Natural History Survey.

Larson, M.A.; Dijak, W.D.; Thompson, F.R., III; Millspaugh, J.J. 2003. **Landscape-level habitat suitability models for twelve species in southern Missouri.** Gen. Tech. Rep. NC-233. St. Paul, MN: U.S. Department of Agriculture, Forest Service, North Central Research Station. 51 p.

Larson, M.A.; Thompson, F.R., III; Millspaugh, J.J.; Dijak, W.D.; Shifley, S.R. 2004. **Linking population viability, habitat suitability, and landscape simulation models for conservation planning.** Ecological Modeling. 180: 103-118.

Liscinsky, S.A. 1972. **The Pennsylvania woodcock management study.** Res. Bull. 171. Harrisburg, PA: Pennsylvania Game Commission. 95 p.

Lynch, J.M. 1981. **Status of the cerulean warbler in the Roanoke River basin of North Carolina.** Chat. 45: 29-35.

Manly, B.F.J.; McDonald, L.L.; Thomas, D.L.; McDonald, T.L.; Erickson, W.P. 2002. **Resource selection by animals: statistical design and analysis for field studies.** Second edition. Dordrecht, The Netherlands: Kluwer Academic Publishers. 221 p.

Marzluff, J.M.; Millspaugh, J.J.; Ceder, K.R.; Oliver, C.D.; Withey, J.; McCarter, J.B.; Mason, C.L.; Comnick, J. 2002. **Modeling changes in wildlife habitat and timber revenues in response to forest management.** Forest Science. 48: 191-202.

Maxson, S J. 1989. **Patterns of activity and home range of hens.** In: Atwater, S.; Schnell, J., eds. Ruffed grouse. Harrisburg, PA: Stackpole Books: 118-129.

Mazur, R. 1996. **Implications of field management for Henslow's sparrow habitat at Saratoga National Historical Park, New York.** Syracuse, NY: State University of New York. 33 p. M.S. thesis.

McCoy, T.D. 2000. **Effects of landscape composition and multi-scale habitat characteristics on the grassland bird community.** Columbia, MO: University of Missouri. 159 p. Ph.D. dissertation.

McDonald, J.E., Jr.; Storm, G.L.; Palmer, W.L. 1998. **Home range and habitat use of male ruffed grouse in managed mixed oak and aspen forest.** Forest Ecology and Management. 109: 271-278.

McNair, D.B.; Post, W. 1993. **Supplement to status and distribution of South Carolina birds.** Contribution No. 8. Charleston, SC: Charleston Museum of Ornithology. 49 p.

Mengel, R.M. 1965. **The birds of Kentucky.** American Ornithologists' Union Ornithological Monographs, No. 3. Lawrence, KS: Allen Press. 581 p.

Menzel, M.A.; Menzel, J.M.; Carter, T.C.; Ford, W.M.; Edwards, J.W. 2001. **Review of the forest habitat relationships of the Indiana Bat (*Myotis sodalis*).** Gen Tech. Rep. NE-284. Newton Square, PA: U.S. Department of Agriculture, Forest Service, Northeastern Research Station. 21 p.

Mueller, A.J.; Twedt, D.J.; Loesch, C.R.; Tripp, K.; Hunter, W.C.; Woodrey, M.S. 2000. **Development of management objectives for breeding birds in the Mississippi Alluvial Valley.** In: Bonney, R., et al., eds. Strategies for bird conservation, proceedings third Partners in Flight international workshop; 1995 Oct. 1-5; Cape May, NJ. RMRS-P-16. Ft. Collins, CO: U.S. Department of Agriculture, Forest Service, Rocky Mountain Research Station.

Murphy, D.W.; Thompson, F.R., III. 1993. **Breeding chronology and habitat of the American Woodcock in Missouri.** In: Longcore, J.R.; Sepik, G.F., eds. Proceedings of the eighth American woodcock symposium. Biological Report 16. Washington, DC: U.S. Fish and Wildlife Service: 12-18.

Nicholson, C.P. 2003. **Ecology of the cerulean warbler in the Cumberland Mountains of east Tennessee.** Knoxville, TN: University of Tennessee. Ph.D. dissertation.

Norman, G.W.; Kirkpatrick, R.L. 1984. **Foods, nutrition, and condition of ruffed grouse in southwestern Virginia.** Journal of Wildlife Management. 48: 183-187.

Osbourne, J.D.; Anderson, J.T.; Spurgeon, A.B. 2005. **Effects of habitat on small-mammal diversity and abundance in West Virginia.** Wildlife Society Bulletin. 33: 814-822.

Pagen, R.W.; Thompson, F.R., III; Burhans, D.E. 2000. **Breeding and post-breeding habitat use by forest migrant songbirds in the Missouri Ozarks.** Condor. 102: 738-747.

Peterjohn, B.G.; Rice, D.L. 1991. **The Ohio breeding atlas.** Columbus, OH: Ohio Department of Natural Resources. 416 p.

Pruitt, L. 1996. **Henslow's sparrow status assessment.** Bloomington, IN: U.S. Fish and Wildlife Service. 109 p. Available at: http://www.fws.gov/midwest/eco_serv/soc/birds/hesp-sa.pdf

Reinert, H.K. 1984a. **Habitat separation between sympatric snake populations.** Ecology. 65: 478-486.

Reinert, H.K. 1984b. **Habitat variation within sympatric snake populations.** Ecology. 65: 1673-1682.

Reinert, H.K.; Zappalorti, R.T. 1988. **Timber rattlesnakes (*Crotalus horridus*) of the Pine Barrens: their movement patterns and habitat preference.** Copeia. 1988: 964-978.

Robbins, C.S.; Dawson, D.K.; Dowell, B.A. 1989. **Habitat area requirements of breeding forest birds of the middle Atlantic states.** Wildlife Monographs. 103: 1-34.

Robbins, C.S.; Fitzpatrick, J.W.; Hamel, P.B. 1992. **A warbler in trouble: *Dendroica cerulea*.** In: Hagan, J.M., III; Johnson, D.W., eds. Ecology and conservation of neotropical migrant landbirds. Washington, DC: Smithsonian Institute Press: 549-562.

Robinson, W.D.; Robinson, S.K. 1999. **Effects of selective logging on forest bird populations in a fragmented landscape.** Conservation Biology. 13: 58-66.

Rodewald, A.D.; Vitz, A.C. 2005. **Edge- and area-sensitivity of shrubland birds.** Journal of Wildlife Management. 69: 681-688.

Rodgers, A.R. 2001. **Recent telemetry technology.** In: Millspaugh J.J.; Marzluff, J.M., eds. Radio tracking and animal populations. San Diego, CA: Academic Press: 79-121.

Rodgers, R.D. 1980. **Ecological relationships of ruffed grouse in southwestern Wisconsin.** Transactions of the Wisconsin Academy of Sciences, Arts and Letters. 68: 97-105.

Rommé, R.C.; Tyrell, K.; Brack, V., Jr. 1995. **Literature summary and habitat suitability index model: components of summer habitat for the Indiana bat, *Myotis sodalis*.** Final report to Indiana Department of Natural Resources. Cincinnati, OH: 3D/Environmental. 190 p. [Unpublished wildlife report, Federal Aid in Wildlife Restoration Project E-1-7, Study No. 8.]

Roseberry, J.L. 1964. **Some responses of bobwhites to snow cover in southern Illinois.** Journal of Wildlife Management. 28: 244-249.

Roseberry, J.L. 1993. **Bobwhite and the "new" biology.** In: Church, K.E.; Dailey, T.V., eds. Proceedings of the third national quail symposium; 1992 July 14-17; Kansas City, MO. Pratt, KS: Kansas Dept. of Wildlife and Parks: 16-20.

Roseberry, J.L.; Klimstra, W.D. 1984. **Population ecology of the bobwhite.** Carbondale, IL: Southern Illinois University Press. 259 p.

Roseberry, J.L.; Sudkamp, S.D. 1998. **Assessing the suitability of landscapes for northern bobwhite.** Journal of Wildlife Management. 62: 895-902.

Rosenberg, K.V.; Barker, S.E.; Rohrbaugh, R.W. 2000. **An atlas of cerulean warbler populations.** Final Report to USFWS: 1997-2000 breeding seasons. Ithaca, NY: Cornell University Laboratory of Ornithology. 56 p.

Roth, R.R.; Johnson, M.S.; Underwood, T.J. 1996. **Wood thrush (*Hylocichla mustelina*).** In: Poole, A.; Gill, F., eds. The Birds of North America. Vol. 7, No. 246. Philadelphia, PA: The Birds of North America, Inc. 28 p.

Rusch, D.H.; DeStefano, S.; Reynolds, M.C.; Lauten, D. 2000. **Ruffed grouse, (*Bonasa umbellus*).** In: Poole, A.; Gill, F., eds. The Birds of North America. Vol. 13, No. 515. Philadelphia, PA: The Birds of North America, Inc. 28 p.

Samson, F.B. 1980. **Island biogeography and the conservation of prairie birds.** Proceedings of the North American Prairie Conference. 7: 293-305.

Schorger, A.W. 1927. **Notes on the distribution of some Wisconsin birds.** I. The Auk. 44: 235-240.

Schroeder, R.L. 1985. **Habitat suitability index models: northern bobwhite.** Biological Rep. 82(10.104). Washington, DC: U.S. Fish and Wildlife Service. 32 p.

Sealy, J.B. 2002. **Ecology and behavior of the timber rattlesnake (*Crotalus horridus*) in the upper Piedmont of North Carolina: identified threats and conservation recommendations.** In: Schuett, G.W., et al., eds. Biology of the vipers. Eagle Mountain, UT: Eagle Mountain Publishing: 561-578.

Seigel, R.A.; Pilgrim, M.A. 2002. **Long-term changes in movement patterns of massasaugas (*Sistrurus catenatus*).** In: Schuett, G.W., et al., eds. Biology of the vipers. Eagle Mountain, UT: Eagle Mountain Publishing: 405-412.

Sekgororoane, G.B.; Dilworth, T.G. 1995. **Relative abundance, richness, and diversity of small** mammals at induced forest edges. Canadian Journal of Zoology. 73: 1432-1437.

Sepik, G.F.; Derleth, E.L. 1993. **Habitat use, home range size, and patterns of moves of the American Woodcock in Maine.** In: Longcore, J.R.; Sepik, G.F., eds. Proceedings of the eighth woodcock symposium. Biological Report 16. Washington, DC: U.S. Fish and Wildlife Service: 41-49.

Sepik, G.F.; McAuley, D.G.; Longcore, J.R. 1993. **Critical review of the current knowledge of the biology of the American woodcock and its management on the breeding grounds.** In: Longcore, J.R.; Sepik, G.F., eds. Proceedings of the eighth woodcock symposium. Biological Report 16. Washington, DC: U.S. Fish and Wildlife Service: 98-104.

Shugart, H.H., Jr.; James, D. 1973. **Ecological succession of breeding bird populations in northwestern Arkansas.** The Auk. 90: 62-77.

Skinner, R.M.; Baskett, T.S.; Blenden, M.D. 1984. **Bird habitat on Missouri prairies.** Terrestrial Series 14. Jefferson City, MO: Missouri Department of Conservation. 37 p.

Smith, C.R. 1992. **Henslow's sparrow *Ammodramus henslowii*.** In: Schneider, K.J.; Pence, D.M., eds. Migratory nongame birds of management concern in the Northeast. Newton Corner, MA: U.S. Fish and Wildlife Service: 315-330.

Smith, D.J.; Smith, C.R. 1992. **Henslow's sparrow and grasshopper sparrow: a comparison of habitat use in Finger Lakes National Forest, New York.** Bird Observer. 20: 187-194.

Stoddard, H.L. 1931. **The bobwhite quail: its life history and management.** New York: Charles Scribner's Sons. 559 p.

Straw, J.A., Jr.; Wakeley, J.S.; Hudgins, J.E.. 1986. **A model for management of diurnal habitat for American woodcock in Pennsylvania.** Journal of Wildlife Management. 50: 378-383.

Sullivan, N.H. 2001. **An algorithm for a landscape level model of mast production.** Columbia, MO: University of Missouri. 293 p. Ph.D. dissertation.

Swengel, S.R. 1996. **Management response of three species of declining sparrows in tallgrass prairie.** Bird Conservation International. 6: 241-253.

Thompson, F.R., III; Dijak, W.D.; Kulowiec, T.G.; Hamilton, D.A. 1992. **Breeding bird populations in Missouri Ozark forests with and without clearcutting.** Journal of Wildlife Management. 56: 23-30.

Thompson, F.R., III; Fritzell, E.K. 1986. **Fall foods and nutrition of ruffed grouse in Missouri.** Transactions of the Missouri Academy of Science. 20: 45-48.

Thompson, F.R., III; Fritzell, E.K. 1988. **Ruffed grouse winter roost site preference and influence on energy demands.** Journal of Wildlife Management. 52: 454-460.

Thompson, F.R., III; Fritzell, E.K. 1989. **Habitat use, home range, and survival of territorial male ruffed grouse.** Journal of Wildlife Management. 53: 15-21.

Todd, W.E.C. 1893. **Summer birds of Indiana and Clearfield counties, Pennsylvania.** The Auk. 10: 35-46.

Torrey, B. 1896. **Virginia notes.** The Auk. 13: 179.

U.S. Fish and Wildlife Service. 1980. **Habitat evaluation procedures (HEP).** Division of Ecological Services Manual 102. Washington, DC: U.S. Fish and Wildlife Service.

U.S. Fish and Wildlife Service. 1981. **Standards for the development of habitat suitability index models for use in the habitat evaluation procedure.** Division of Ecological Services Manual 103. Washington, DC: U.S. Fish and Wildlife Service.

Van Kley, J.E.; Parker, G.R.; Franzmeier, D.P.; Randolph, J.C. 1994. **Field guide: ecological classification** of the Hoosier National Forest and surrounding areas of Indiana. Bedford, IN: U.S. Department of Agriculture, Forest Service, Hoosier National Forest. 79 p.

Vega Rivera, J.H.; Rappole, J.H.; McShea, W.J.; Haas, C.A. 1998. **Wood thrush postfledging movements and habitat use in northern Virginia.** The Condor. 100: 69-78.

Walker, Z.J. 2000. **The spatial ecology of the timber rattlesnake (*Crotalus horridus*) in south central Indiana.** West Lafayette, IN: Purdue University. 45 p. M.S. thesis.

Weakland, C.A.; Wood, P.B. 2002. **Cerulean warbler (*Dendroica cerulea*) microhabitat characteristics and landscape-level habitat characteristics in southern West Virginia in relation to mountaintop mining/valley fills.** Final Project Report to U.S. Geological Survey, Biological Resources Division, Species At Risk Program. Morgantown, VA: West Virginia Cooperative Fish and Wildlife Research Unit and West Virginia University, Division of Forestry. 55 p.

Wenny, D.G.; Clawson, R.L.; Faaborg, J.; Sheriff, S.L. 1993. **Population density, habitat selection and minimum area requirements of three forest-interior warblers in central Missouri.** Condor. 95: 968-979.

Widmann, O. 1895a. **Swainson's warbler an inhabitant of the swampy woods of southeastern Missouri.** The Auk. 12: 112-117.

Widmann, O. 1895b. **The brown creeper nesting in the cypress swamp of southeastern Missouri.** The Auk. 12: 350-355.

Widmann, O. 1897. **The summer home of Bachman's warbler no longer unknown.** The Auk. 14: 305-309.

Wiggers, E.P.; Laubhan, H.K.; Hamilton, D.A. 1992. **Forest structure associated with ruffed grouse**

abundance. Forest Ecology and Management. 49: 211-218.

Williams, C.K ; Lutz, R.S.; Applegate, R.D.; Rusch, D.H. 2000. **Habitat use and survival of northern bobwhite (Colinus virginianus) in cropland and rangeland ecosystems during the hunting season.** Canadian Journal of Zoology. 78: 1562-1566.

Winter, M. 1999. **Nesting biology of Dickcissels and Henslow's sparrows in southwestern Missouri prairie fragments.** Wilson Bulletin. 111: 515-526.

Winter, M.; Faaborg, J. 1999. **Patterns of area sensitivity in grassland-nesting birds.** Conservation Biology. 13: 1424-1436.

Winter, M.; Johnson, D.H.; Faaborg, J. 2000. **Evidence for edge effects on multiple levels in tallgrass prairie.** The Condor. 102: 256-266.

Wishart, R.A.; Bider, J.R. 1976. **Habitat preference of woodcock in southwestern Quebec.** Journal of Wildlife Management. 40: 523-531.

Wood, P.B.; Bosworth, S.B.; Dettmers, R. 2003. **Cerulean warbler relative abundance and frequency of occurrence relative to large-scale edge.** Condor. 108: 154-165.

Woodward. A.A.; Fink, A.D.; Thompson, F.R., III. 2001. **Edge effects and ecological traps: effects on shrubland birds in Missouri.** Journal of Wildlife Management. 65: 668-675.

Woolf, A.; Norris, R.; Kube, J. 1984. **Evaluation of ruffed grouse introductions in southern Illinois.** In: Robinson, W.L., ed.; Ruffed grouse management: state of the art in the early 1980's. Symposium proceedings, 45th Midwest Fish and Wildlife Conference; 1983 December 5-7; St. Louis, MO. Bloomington, IN: Wildlife Society and Ruffed Grouse Society, North Central Section: 59-74.